In Search of Ernst

Discovering the Unspoken Fate of the Königsgartens

by
Michael Garton

ISBN: 978-1-916732-09-4

First Edition published in Great Britain in 2015 by
Horsgate ● Oxford

Copyright 2023

All rights reserved. No part of this publication may be reproduced, stored in a retrieval system or transmitted in any form or by any means, electronic, mechanical, photocopy, recording or otherwise, without prior written consent of the copyright owner. Nor can it be circulated in any form of binding or cover other than that in which it is published and without similar condition including this condition being imposed on a subsequent purchaser.
The right of Michael Garton to be identified as the author of this work has been asserted in accordance with the Copyright Designs and Patents Act 1988.
A copy of this book is deposited with the British Library

This edition Published By: -

i2i Publishing. Manchester.
www.i2ipublishing.co.uk

In memory of Ernst Königsgarten. He chose Altaussee as his last resting-place yet died in Theresienstadt in 1942

Dedication

To my children and grandchildren

Acknowledgements

I wish to thank the following for their help and encouragement during the writing of this book:

Thea Bentley, the last family survivor of my father's generation, who has kept alive for me that link with the past;

Ursula Kals-Friese, who knew my grandfather's house in Altaussee at a time when some of his belongings were still there;

Carole Angier, who was interested enough in Ernst's memorial plaque in Altaussee to research and write about it;

Leo Walkner, who had written about my grandfather before he had met me, and gave me vital introductions to the Austrian Records Office;

Tessa Garton, my sister, who typed up the original manuscript;

Antonia Brotchie, who painstakingly translated many pages of indecipherable German handwriting;

Mark Holland, who visited Theresienstadt with me and helped me with the first publication of this book, and above all

Bridget Geddes, without whose endless enthusiasm, support and forbearance this book would never have been written.

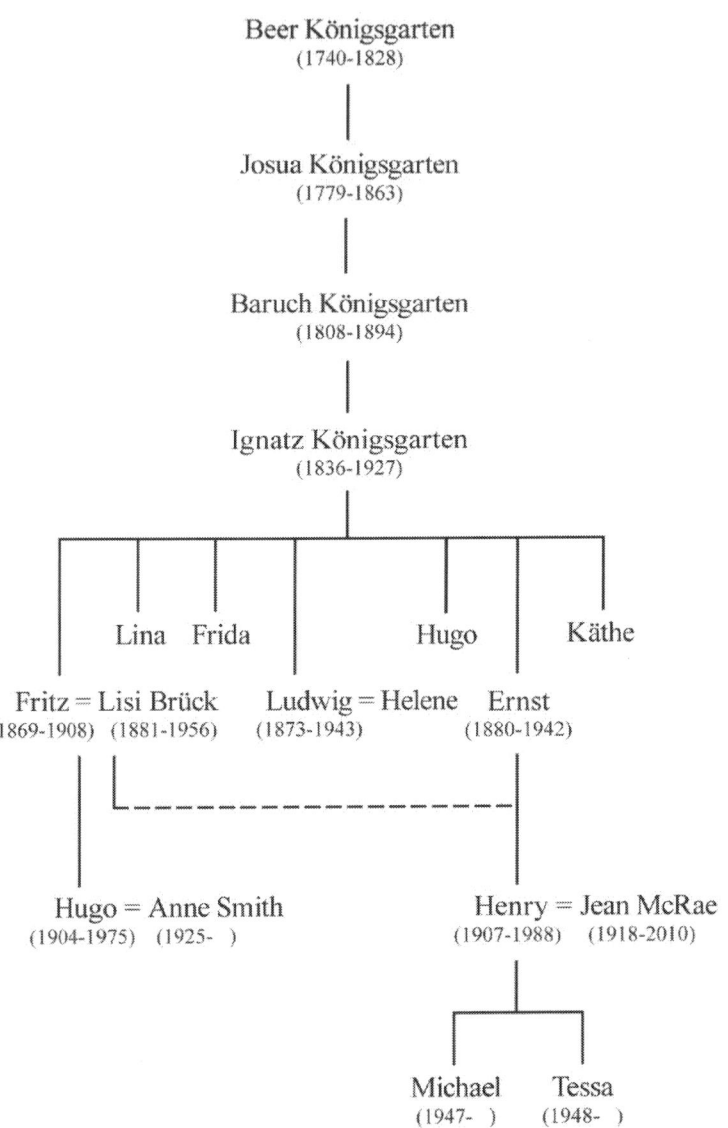

Chronology

28 Dec 1836	Ignatz Königsgarten born
2 Dec 1848	*Accession of Franz Joseph to the throne of the Austro-Hungarian Empire*
11 Nov 1869	Fritz Königsgarten born
31 Aug 1873	Ludwig Königsgarten born
14 July 1880	Ernst Königsgarten born
7 Aug 1881	Lisi Brück born
5 April 1903	Marriage of Fritz and Lisi in Brno
13 April 1904	Hugo Königsgarten born
16 May 1907	Heinrich (Henry) Königsgarten born
1907	*Klimt finishes first portrait of Adele Bloch-Bauer*
18 Jan 1908	Fritz Königsgarten dies
1911	Lisi, Hugo and Henry move to Vienna. Ernst follows
1912	*Klimt finishes second portrait of Adele Bloch-Bauer*
28 June 1914	*Assassination of Archduke Franz Ferdinand*
4 Aug 1914	*Britain declares war on Germany*
1 April 1915	Lisi marries Max Bohne and moves to Berlin with Hugo and Henry

21 Nov 1916	*Emperor Franz Joseph dies*
25 Oct 1917	*Bolshevik Revolution in Russia, led by Lenin*
6 Feb 1918	*Klimt dies*
11 Nov 1918	*Armistice signed with Germany*
28 June 1919	*Treaty of Versailles - Czechoslovakia created*
24 Jan 1925	Adele Bloch-Bauer dies
19 Oct 1927	Ignatz Königsgarten dies
Dec 1929	Henry first arrives in London
1931	Henry moves to Paris
27 Feb 1933	*Reichstag fire*
5 March 1933	*Hitler comes to power*
23 Mar 1933	*'Enabling Act' passed giving Hitler absolute power*
16 April 1933	Lisi moves back to Vienna. Hugo follows
January 1934	Max joins Lisi in Vienna
30 June 1934	*'The Night of the Long Knives' - mass arrests and killing of Hitler's opponents*
19 Aug 1934	*Hitler combines offices of President and Chancellor*
3 June 1937	Thea marries Robert Bloch-Bauer
28 Oct 1937	Henry returns to London to join Hart Son & Co., merchant bankers
12 Mar 1938	*Hitler invades Austria (the 'Anschluss')*

13 Mar 1938	Hugo flees Austria
30 Aug 1938	Lisi flees Austria
29 Sept 1938	*'Munich Agreement' signed*
October 1938	*Hitler occupies the Sudetenland*
20 Oct 1938	Thea and Robert flee Austria
9 Nov 1938	*'Kristallnacht'*
20 Nov 1938	Ernst moves back to Brno
16 Mar 1939	*Hitler occupies rest of Czechoslovakia*
1 Sept 1939	*Hitler invades Poland*
3 Sept 1939	*Britain and France declare war on Germany*
22 June 1941	*Hitler invades Russia*
5 Dec 1941	Ernst deported to Theresienstadt
16 Dec 1941	The firm Ig. Königsgarten 'Aryanised'
15 Jan 1942	Ernst dies in Theresienstadt
20 Jan 1942	*Wannsee Conference decides on 'Final Solution'*
23 Mar 1942	Lisi's mother Eugenie deported to Theresienstadt
4 April 1942	Ludwig deported to Theresienstadt
15 April 1942	Lisi's mother Eugenie dies in Theresienstadt
4 June 1942	*Reinhard Heydrich ('Reichsprotektor of Bohemia and Moravia') assassinated*
20 Aug 1942	Max deported to Theresienstadt
8 Nov 1942	*US enters war in Europe*

23 July 1943	Max dies in Theresienstadt
3 Sept 1943	*Italy surrenders to the Allies*
15 Dec 1943	Ludwig transferred from Theresienstadt to Auschwitz, where he dies
22 Jan 1944	*Allies land at Anzio, Italy*
6 June 1944	*D-Day Landings*
16 Nov 1944	Henry marries Jean McRae
March 1945	Henry posted to Hamburg
30 April 1945	*Hitler commits suicide*
8 May 1945	*VE Day - Germany surrenders*
10 May 1945	*Altaussee liberated* Henry takes over German radio station in Flensburg
15 Aug 1945	*VJ Day - Japan surrenders* Jean Garton posted to Hamburg
21 Aug 1945	Henry formally recovers the Villa Königsgarten
October 1945	Henry 'de-mobbed' and returns to London
13 Nov 1945	Ferdinand Bloch-Bauer dies
January 1946	Jean 'de-mobbed' and returns to London
16 Dec 1946	Henry granted British nationality
15 Mar 1947	Michael Garton born
29 July 1948	Tessa Garton born

1 Aug 1949	Gaiswinkler gives Henry a copy of his book
25 Aug 1956	Lisi Bohne-Königsgarten dies
23 June 1975	Hugo Garten dies
1 Aug 1988	Henry Garton dies
9 Nov 1989	*Berlin Wall re-opened - leading to re-unification of Germany*
16 Jan 2006	Maria Altmann recovers Klimt paintings
14 Aug 2010	Jean Garton dies
7 Feb 2011	Maria Altmann dies

Note

Shortly after he settled in England Henry Königsgarten shortened his name to Henry Garten, but was later advised by the Army to anglicise it still further to Henry Garton. His brother Hugo, who did not join the Army, retained the 'e' and therefore adopted the name Hugo Garten. Their mother Lisi combined the surnames of her two husbands and therefore adopted the surname Bohne-Königsgarten.

Table of Contents

Acknowledgements v

Chronology ix

Preface xvi

Chapter One: The Search Begins 1

Chapter Two: Altaussee 9

Chapter Three: The National Archives 32

Chapter Four: Between the Wars 57

Chapter Five: Vienna 83

Chapter Six: Theresienstadt 99

Chapter Seven: The 'Alpine Fortress' 107

Chapter Eight: Central European Trip 2014 119

Appendix I: Last Days in Vienna 147

Appendix II: Lisi's Diary 165

Appendix III: Flensburg Letter 189

Appendix IV: Gerda 193

Preface

I was born on 15 March 1947. That winter had been one of the worst on record for many years, and when my mother went into Queen Charlotte's Hospital to give birth there was still snow on the ground in central London. At that time my parents were living in 41 Hasker Street in Chelsea. They had been married in November 1944 but this was their first married home after returning to civilian life after the war. In July 1948 my sister Tessa was born and shortly after that we moved to 8 Moore Street which was a more spacious house just around the corner.

I cannot be precise about the date of my earliest memories. I must have been about three. I remember the nursery school I went to in Cadogan Gardens, run by Miss de Brissac. (Her name always sounded like Mr Brissac, and I could never understand why she was referred to as 'Mr'!) My mother subsequently told me that she had been a member of the French Resistance during the war. Anyway, she had this small nursery school round the corner from our house, and I remember being placed amongst much bigger girls for French singing as apparently I had a good French accent!

Life was comfortable and secure. We did not venture far from the heart of Chelsea – north to Hyde Park, south to the Royal Hospital Gardens, east to St James's Park and west to South Kensington. Our shopping was done very locally. Groceries were bought from Oakshott's in Milner Street, and if they were too heavy to carry home, they were brought round by a delivery boy on a bicycle. In the same street there was also a greengrocer, run by a very educated Hungarian lawyer who had fled his home country (I realised this had something to do with the war but wasn't sure what), a dairy (United Dairies), an ironmonger's (Mr Holland), a stationer's (Miss Watson), and A May & Sons the builders, not to mention a pub (The Australian). In Cadogan Street there was a chemist (Mr Green), a dry cleaners (Sketchley's), and Mr Cianfarini who sold home-made

Italian ice-cream. Just about everything else was bought from Peter Jones or Harrods, both less than ten minutes' walk away. There was a butcher opposite Peter Jones on one side, a branch of Lloyds Bank on the other, and Kings Road consisted mainly of shoe shops and vegetable shops, and of course Woolworth's (but that was always considered rather down-market!). There was a Post Office on Chelsea Green, where ration books were issued, and most importantly, as I grew older, where Hornby Dublo was sold and where I bought all my electric trains, and another ironmonger's (Mr Simmonds) whose whole shop appeared to be held up by the pots and pans that he sold. There was also free orange juice for children available from the nearby clinic, for this was still the immediate post-war period and rationing continued for some items until the early 1950s.

But of course, although the war was mentioned frequently by the grown-ups, it was usually in the context of 'since the war' or 'before the war', and nothing was actually ever said <u>about</u> the war; nor do I remember asking about it, or if I did, nothing interesting ever came of it.

There were however numerous signs everywhere of war damage, but as a child one just took these for granted without really considering the trauma that lay behind them. There were gaps in the streets where houses had once stood, and where the neighbouring houses were then propped up by large wooden buttresses, and further afield there were large open areas of wasteland which just lay bare or were used as car parks.

There were however very few cars around. When we first got a car in 1952 (passed down by an aunt of my mother's), I distinctly remember at times it being one of only three parked in the street. But this is slightly misleading, because most people, including my parents, initially kept their cars in the mews garages nearby. Ours was generally only used at weekends and my parents would ask the garage man to have it ready for such-and-such a date or time, and it would be 'got out' ready for them to collect, for in the garage itself the cars were just put in one behind the other, with no space in between.

But cars were not the only form of transport. The milk was delivered daily by horse and cart (the stables were behind the dairy round the corner), and the 'rag-and-bone man' came by from time to time with his rather scruffier horse and cart, collecting 'any old iron' and other unwanted items. It took me a long time to fathom out his distinctive call, but eventually I did. It went: 'Any old ancient or ordinary lumber.' I can still hear it to this day, with the emphasis firmly placed rather strangely on the second syllable of 'lumber'. But it was the milkman's horse who impressed us the most, as he completely understood the milkman's round, and he would walk forward, stop, start again, and turn left or right at the top of the street entirely on command, without the milkman so much as touching him.

There was also the French onion man. Twice a year he would come by with his bicycle strung with strings of Breton onions, and we inevitably bought some. He told me later that he came with several tons of onions, and rented a shed somewhere near Waterloo Station where he kept them and from where he wheeled his bicycle every day laden with strings.

Coal was delivered in hundredweight sacks from the back of a flat-bed lorry. Twenty hundredweight sacks was the usual delivery, and every house had a coalhole in the pavement outside it into which they were tipped, and the empty sacks then placed back on the lorry neatly folded in half. The coalmen always carried a broom and swept the pavement when they had finished. Most houses had coal-fired boilers, and this was the sole method of heating the hot water. There were no radiators, only open coal (or gas) fires, so a good supply of coal was essential.

The dustmen came once every few weeks. There were three or four of them to a team. Every bin had to be lifted up from the 'area' below street level onto a dustman's shoulder and then manually emptied onto the dustcart (which had about four up-and-over sliding doors on each side), and then put back under the steps in the 'area', so it was not lightweight work. The dustcart was drawn by a three-wheeled Scammell Scarab tractor unit, much loved by British Railways and other urban transporters of goods as they were very manoeuvrable.

Cadogan Square had a large private garden in the middle, to which local residents could (for a fee) acquire a key, and from an early age we were taken there, first in a pram, then on foot, and later with little tricycles or bikes. Occasionally we would be left there, under the eye of one of the many (uniformed and rather fierce) nannies who happened to be there with their charges. There was a head gardener, Mr Nash, who would make sure the bigger children all behaved, whom

The author aged 6 in Cadogan Square gardens (in a Hill House jersey)

we found rather stern when we were young. The gardens had a tennis court, on which I initially had tennis lessons and then used a lot in my early teens.

This, then, was the self-contained world in which I grew up. I went to Miss de Brissac's from the age of three to five, and then to Hill House in Hans Place in the spring of 1952 until 1955. A few of my memories of Hill House can be found in the biography of Col. Townend written by Neil Sullivan in 2011 entitled *The King of Hans Place*, to which I contributed in a small way. It was a friendly and thoroughly inspiring school, entirely due to the exceptional talents of Col. Townend, and I have nothing but good memories of it. When I was 11, Col. Townend started taking 'old boys' skiing on the Rochers de Naye above Montreux in Switzerland, and so for three consecutive years I spent two weeks every Christmas holidays learning to ski under his tuition. In the 1930s he himself had been a very proficient skier and athlete at Olympic level.

But what of my parents? My mother was English, of Scottish and Irish descent. Her father had been in the Indian Army throughout his professional life and as a result my mother had lived in India for the first few years of her life. When my grandfather retired she grew up in Devon. During the war she served as a VAD. The Voluntary Aid Detachment was a voluntary unit providing field nursing services to the army, mainly in military hospitals, and came into its own during both world wars as a supplement to the overstretched professional nursing services. After spending the first years of the war in hospitals mainly on the south coast, dealing with wounded soldiers repatriated to England, my mother followed the advancing Allies into Belgium and Germany after D-Day. In this capacity she ended up in a British Military Hospital in Hamburg in August 1945 where she remained until she was demobbed in January 1946. When I was a child she seemed to me so completely at home in London, that it is hard to recognise that in fact she had only lived in London for just over a year when I was born, and that furthermore until that time she had been nursing in a war-time or war-torn environment very different to the Chelsea life I grew up to know.

My father's life had seen even more dramatic changes, although none of this was of course apparent to me in my childhood. By coincidence he too had spent the last months of his war-time military career in Hamburg. He had been posted there in March 1945 as part of what was known as Information Control, a unit set up to try and re-establish normal life in Germany after its defeat. Husbands and wives were not in fact supposed to be stationed in the same place, but somehow in my parents' case this seems to have been overlooked, and they were in no hurry to point it out! My father returned to civilian life in October 1945 and resumed his position with a merchant bank in the City where he had held a partnership before the war. He had worked in the City from 1937 to 1940 so in fact he knew London very well. It was not therefore difficult for him to re-establish himself. But this belies completely the nature of the life which he had experienced before that, all the challenges and hardships of which were of course unknown to us as children. I saw my father go to work in his pin-striped suit every day, with his bowler hat, briefcase and brolly. Before he had even turned the corner of the street he had usually been joined by at least two other 'City gents' from neighbouring houses, and so he seemed completely part of that 'Establishment'. He left the house at 9 o'clock to walk to Sloane Square Underground Station, where he bought his return ticket to Mansion House - which when I was a bit older cost 2/6d (12p in today's money) – and returned every evening at 6 or 6.30, almost like clockwork. It all seemed perfectly safe and sound. But his life had not always been like that.

There was one difference which I could detect from quite an early age between my father and most of the so-called Establishment – my father spoke with a German accent, and in my early days at any rate he would even speak German to his mother and brother. Although it was some time before we as children really became aware of this, our friends however would have noticed it immediately. But he was not the only one with an accent. My parents had a good number of friends who also seemed to have a foreign past, and gradually I became aware that most of them had been forced by some kind of pre-war political crisis to leave their native Austria or Germany and come to England.

Naturally, as we grew up I learnt a bit more about the places where my father had grown up and lived, but it was more a matter of dates and places than anything deeper. I also became able to place the dates of his movements in their historical context, but as for the underlying reasons for these moves we were told virtually nothing, and as will be apparent from the following account, we also asked very little too. The position did not really change as we grew older. My father died when I was 41, so he was no longer there to ask after that, but I didn't ask my mother either. She died when I was 63 and I was still little the wiser as to my father's family past. I was 64 before I began to discover a bit of the world of his childhood and youth, a story so dominated by evil and persecution that it had been kept from us as children, and perhaps would have been kept from us forever, had it not been for a few surviving records in the attic. This, then, is the background to the following account.

Chapter One: The Search Begins

Incredible as it may seem, I knew next to nothing of my father's family until I started this family research in 2011. It might be thought that had my father lived longer (he died in 1988) and not died so unexpectedly, he might at some stage have told me more about his past, or I might have brought the subject up myself, but I think this would have been unlikely. I think (now) that for his part he had decided to put his whole family past behind him, and for my part the fact that I never raised the subject with my mother probably indicates that I would not have done so with my father either. All of which is most regrettable.

What we knew from an early age was that my father Henry had been born in Brno, then part of Austria, in 1907, that his father Fritz had died when he was about six months old, after which he had grown up very close to his uncle Ernst who had treated him like a son. We had been told that Ernst had come to London at some stage where he had suffered an eye injury, but that he had been so well treated at Moorfields Eye Hospital that he had said to Henry "When you grow up, you must go to England". Unlikely as that might seem for a reason, it was affirmed many a time and we accepted it. And we knew that Ernst had been a great fencer. There may have been some mention of the Olympics (my sister Tessa, who also took up fencing, remembers this more) but it was very vague.

We knew that when my father was four, the family had moved to Vienna, and we vaguely knew that his mother Lisi had later married a Berliner called Max who subsequently had also died. We knew that in 1930, following Ernst's advice, my father came to England for the first time, but that he then spent five years in Paris before returning to England for good in 1937. We had been told that his mother Lisi and brother Hugo had left Austria in 1938 after the arrival of the Nazis (not because they were Jewish, but because they were 'anti-Hitler'), but that

Ernst had been deported to Theresienstadt (again because he was 'anti-Hitler') where he had died. Those were the bones of what we knew.

The subsequent process of further discovery all began over Christmas 2010. Our mother had recently died and Tessa and I were clearing out her attic. One of the items there was a large leather trunk, covered in dust, inside which was a black metal box of old family papers. As neither of these were easy items to get down the step-ladder, they got left till the very last. When we did get them down and opened the metal box and found it to be full of documents in German, we closed the lid pretty quickly and decided it was a task for another day. So it was not until some months later, after I had moved to Swerford, that I began to investigate the contents.

One of the first items I came across was a 'chronicle' written by my great-grandfather Ignatz in 1916, which contained a few paragraphs on each member of the family from the time the name Königsgarten was first adopted. I say 'adopted' because this is what happened. In 1797 the then Emperor Joseph II decreed that in order to put Jews on the same footing as non-Jews, they should all adopt a surname. Until then they had traditionally had none. This was not a form of persecution; quite the contrary. Joseph II was a man of enlightenment and wanted to end religious persecution by putting the Jewish community on equal terms with all others. It was up to them what surname they chose. As we know, many adopted the name of their profession or the town where they lived. My ancestor, however, took the name of the local squire. I can do no better than quote from the 'chronicle':

'The first Jew who took the family name Königsgarten on a permanent basis was Reb Beer Blasowitz. Reb indicated his citizen's title, Beer was his true name and Blasowitz (now Blažovice) was the place where he lived, a town near Austerlitz. The squire/lord of the manor of Blasowitz at that time was called Königsgarten. When asked by the well-liked Reb Beer Blasowitz whether he could adopt and use the same name as the good squire, the latter granted him his request.'

And that, according to Ignatz, is how the name Königsgarten came to be the family name.

Beer (a nickname for Bernard) was born in 1740. After acquiring his new name he moved to Bučowice, also in Moravia, and acquired the Liechtenstein brandy establishment. Beer had four children, the oldest of whom was a son named Josua. Josua inherited the brandy business which in turn he passed on to his eldest son Baruch. Bridget and I visited the magnificent, but now rather derelict, Liechtenstein castle where the brewery was based (but without at that time knowing the family connection), on our tour of Moravian country houses in May 2011. Baruch's second son was my great-grandfather Ignatz, born in 1836.

Brno (or Brünn in German) is the capital of the region called Moravia which until 1918 had formed part of the Austro-Hungarian Empire. That Empire came to an end with the Treaty of Versailles in 1919 at the end of the First World War when the country of Czechoslovakia was created, consisting of Moravia, Bohemia and Silesia. More recently Czechoslovakia split peacefully into the Czech Republic, with its capital Prague, and Slovakia, with its capital Bratislava.

So, in early 2011, by means of this 'chronicle', I discovered a complete family tree from 1740 down to my father (who was 9 at the time the chronicle was written). I had always been told that my great-grandfather Ignatz had had some kind of factory in Brno (the home of the Bren gun – the name a combination of Brno and Enfield, as in Lee-Enfield), but now I had the full details. Ignatz had established under his own name a sheet metal business. I can do no better than quote again from Ignatz's chronicle, where he described himself and his business in the following terms:

'Aged 13 and 14 he (Ignatz) *studied at the technical school, and when he was 15 took a commercial course at a similar institution in Brünn. Aged 16 he took over the running of his father's sawmill and timber business in Lillenschitz. Aged 20 he set up on his own and carried on a business in artificial and natural wool. In 1878 he set up*

a sheet metal factory, principally for the sugar industry, raw materials, sugar cubes etc. At the same time he took part in the construction of barracks, water pipes, various railway works and other miscellaneous undertakings.'

But the most dramatic fact that the chronicle established was that my father must have known his grandfather Ignatz, as never at any time had I heard my father mention him. Ignatz had clearly lived until at least 1916. Subsequent investigation revealed that he did not die until 1927, by which time my father would have been 20, so it is inconceivable that he did not know him well. In fact I now believe that my father had even been born in his house. Yet he had never spoken of him!

This, in itself, might not seem a particularly significant discovery, but it was, because it raised several questions. If there was one family member of whom he had never spoken, were there others? When he first came to England in 1930, what members of his family did he leave behind? When Lisi and Hugo fled to England in 1938, were there other family members apart from Ernst who stayed behind? Finally, why the silence about the past? Was it because they were Jewish? This had never really been spoken of, but from the chronicle it was quite clear that the family were Jewish. Perhaps Ernst had died in a concentration camp not because he was 'anti-Hitler', as we had been told, but because he was Jewish? And is that why Hugo and his mother left in 1938? And what happened to the family house in Brno, etc., etc.? All these questions needed an answer.

My father therefore had clearly known his paternal grandfather well, but not so his paternal grandmother, Emilie, who had died before he was born. Ignatz writes the following of her in his usual glowing terms:

'On 6 September 1869 Ignatz married the gentle and generally loved and respected Miss Emilie Kuhn, daughter of Herr Josua and Frau Kuhn from Butschowitz. Mrs Emilie Königsgarten was an excellent housewife, a very worthy/upright spouse and the most beloved mother. She was very charitable and generously/nobly

disposed. After 37 happy years of marriage she died sadly on 14 February 1906 [in fact 1905] *after a short illness, following an apparently well-carried-out operation. She was 59.'*

Unfortunately I know no more about her. But she had produced seven children. The two relevant ones from our point of view are the eldest, Fritz, born in 1869, and the second youngest, Ernst, born in 1880. Although Ignatz writes in glowing terms of every family member, Fritz must have been the apple of his father's eye, as Ignatz's passage on Fritz knows no bounds!:

'He was the justifiable pride of his parents and all his relations. Even in his earliest years he enjoyed rare deep respect and admiration, and was virtually idolised by his circle of friends. His sincerity, his love of the truth and his noble kind-heartedness were proverbial. He was intellectually very gifted, had a unique sense of purpose and hard work, and a well-trained talent for technical, economic and business matters.'

Some write-up! (The passage on Ernst is produced later in this account.) Meanwhile, while I was digesting all this information, and wondering what else may have been hidden from us, another entirely unrelated event happened, but one which would have enormous significance for my enquiries. Someone called Maria Altmann died in Los Angeles in February 2011.

Maria Altmann was the last surviving niece of Adele Bloch-Bauer, whose two portraits by Gustav Klimt are two of the world's most iconic paintings. When one of these paintings (known as *The Lady in Gold*) was sold in 2006 for US $135 million, it was the most expensive painting ever sold. The dramatic story of the seizure of these paintings by the Nazis and their subsequent recovery by Maria nearly 70 years later, which re-hit the world's headlines in 2011 on account of her death, is described at a later point in this account. To explain its significance to my story at this point, I need to introduce a cousin called Thea Bentley.

Thea is a third cousin of my fathers who lives in Vancouver, now aged 105[1], and who was married to Robert Bloch-Bauer, a nephew of Adele and Ferdinand, and thus a sister-in-law of Maria's. Thea and Robert fled Vienna in 1938 and emigrated to Vancouver (where they adopted the surname Bentley). I had known Thea since I was a child – she used to visit England from time to time, and I even stayed with her in Vancouver for a week in my gap year. In recent years, after she grew too old to continue visiting Europe, my mother and she kept in touch by telephone. When my mother died in 2010, I kept in touch in her place. So one day, when I rang her in February 2011, she asked if I had seen the obituaries of Maria Altmann in the papers. Well, unfortunately I knew nothing of Maria Altmann or the famous Klimts, so she explained the whole history and her connection with it.

Suffice it to say for the moment that to recover the paintings Maria had employed the services of a young American lawyer called Randol Schoenberg who, like Maria herself, lived in Los Angeles. Randy was not only a family friend of Maria's but also a distant relation. He is also the grandson of Arnold Schönberg, the composer. Thea suggested I contact him, as he may have more information on the history of the Königsgartens.

So I emailed Randy Schoenberg. Not only did he introduce me to the genealogy website 'Geni', on which he had already put many members of my father's family, but he also said that he was particularly interested to hear from me as he had been trying to trace the original of a libretto manuscript that my uncle Hugo had written for his maternal grandfather Eric Zeisl, also a composer, and he wondered whether I had any

---

[1] Thea was born in 1918 and although very frail and nearly blind she is still in possession of all her mental faculties. I visited her on the occasion of her 100th birthday and I continue to speak to her regularly on the telephone, Needless to say she is the last of that generation still alive.

information as to whether it still existed. I said not off-hand, but that I would make enquiries.

Hugo had died in 1975, but I knew that his wife, my aunt Anne[2], had given all his papers to a department of London University, and from the Internet I was able to establish that this was the Institute for German and Romantic Studies. It was an easy matter to telephone them. I was put through to Andrea Ludowisy. When I mentioned the purpose of my enquiry, she said that it was an extraordinary coincidence but that the boxes containing Hugo's papers were on the floor beside her desk and had been there for some time as she was waiting to find a moment to go through them. This she would now do with an increased sense of urgency (and a heightened degree of interest!).

In due course I visited the Institute and made a number of useful contacts and interesting discoveries, but more of that anon. For the moment, suffice it to say that Andrea rang me back a few days later to say that she had been through the boxes, but sadly they contained no such libretto manuscript. I was able to report back to Randy, but although that enquiry of his had drawn a blank, his work on Geni had completed many family connections. Thanks to Ignatz's chronicle and also a family tree prepared by my mother I was then able to complete many of the remaining blanks. Gradually the family tree was growing.

---

[2] Anne died in 2018

Chapter Two: Altaussee

At this point I need to introduce the reader to the Austrian village of Altaussee. It is where my father's uncle Ernst had a house, and where my father had spent many of his summers in his youth. It is a name which will be familiar to many Austrians and Austrian émigrés, but not necessarily to any foreigner. In 2009 I had re-met Bridget, and she was interested enough in my family history and the connection with Altaussee to be keen to drive there with me for a brief holiday in September 2010. We talked about this with my mother over that summer when she was ill, but by the time we actually went my mother had sadly died. We left in September, shortly after her funeral.

    Altaussee is a small village at the end of a valley, with its own lake, near the spa towns of Bad Aussee and Bad Ischl, in the Austrian lake district near Salzburg called the Salzkammergut. Tessa and I had known the name Altaussee since our earliest childhood – our parents had gone there for a week many summers, taking it in as part of their usual three-week European summer holiday by car – and we went there three times with our parents in the early 1960s, between the ages (in my case) of 13 and 16. It is a village where many Viennese (and particularly Jewish Viennese – not that we realised that) had, or had had, summer holiday houses. Ernst had had a house there too, and my father clearly regarded it as a kind of second home. But, as children, we had not known quite how much of a home it really was. When I was about 15 (during perhaps my second visit to Altaussee), my mother told us one day in semi-hushed tones, that Ernst was not only my father's uncle, but was also in fact his true father. His mother, it seemed, had had a liaison with her brother-in-law shortly before her husband Fritz's death, and our father was the outcome of it.

Altaussee with the Loser behind

Altaussee and the Dachstein Glacier

Although my grandmother Lisi and Ernst had never married, they had remained good friends, and Ernst had therefore managed to treat my father as a son without this raising any eyebrows. Although my uncle Hugo was therefore the son of Lisi and Fritz, my father Henry was in fact the son of Lisi and Ernst. Hugo and Henry were in fact half-brothers. But as to when my father first knew that Ernst was more than just an uncle to him, we never found out. Either we never asked, or if we did, my mother never knew either. This was not a subject we ever discussed with my father. It was never brought up by him, and we never felt it was up to us to bring it up.

So, speaking I think for both of us, Tessa and I had three very happy and memorable family holidays in Altaussee at formative years of our lives; so much so that I went back to Altaussee myself on a number of occasions over the subsequent years. One of these occasions was a family holiday in 1997 which included my mother and Tessa and all of our children.

When we had been to Altaussee with our parents in our youth, we had of course visited the Villa Königsgarten (the name by which Ernst's house is still known). We knew that my father had recovered the house after the war but that he had sold it in about 1947 to Hannah Schiff. She was an Austrian spinster who lived in London but who wanted to return to Austria or anyway spend the summers there. When we visited the house in the 1960s, Miss Schiff was still in residence and I remember her well, a short rather plump woman always dressed in a dirndl, who was very welcoming and who clearly felt at home in Austria.

We had always stayed in the '*Seehotel*' (the *Hotel Am See*), the large hotel at the far end of the village on the edge of the lake (where we also stayed in 1997 when we went for the last time with my mother). It had huge rooms (often with an ante-room or sitting room attached) and even bigger bathrooms, and a number of Austrian émigrés returned there regularly every summer. The hotel had been in the ownership of the Frischmuth family for several generations, and the head waiter was a particularly colourful character whose exaggerated movements as he delved for change from his bulging wallet, we children had particular fun in mimicking.

The Seehotel

Altaussee's setting was particularly beautiful. We would never fail on any visit to walk at least once round the lake, take out one of the local flat-bottomed boats like a punt (called a *Platte*), climb one or two of the local mountains, and go on a number of trips to neighbouring lakes and villages. But on one occasion I distinctly remember my father visiting the local cemetery, on the edge of the lake, close to the hotel, in order to check that the plaque that he had had made in memory of Ernst had been duly installed on the churchyard wall. I was therefore always conscious that there was a plaque to Ernst in the churchyard, and out of a sense of respect, I made a point of looking it out on subsequent visits.

So, when Bridget and I visited Altaussee in 2010, although we were not there for long, I once again made a point of looking into the churchyard to see the plaque. I wanted to show it to Bridget and she wanted to see it. We were staying in the *Seehotel* and as we walked along the lakeside path our first evening we looked into the adjoining churchyard. But there was no sign of the plaque. I wondered what had happened to it.

The next day we went to call in on the Villa Königsgarten. It was a lovely sunny day, one of those rare and perfect Altaussee summer days, even though it was in fact September. The house looked wonderful, with its magnificent Virginia creeper and recessed balconies, the pond full of lilies, the grass a rich green, and a particularly attractive summerhouse in the corner of the garden. I rang the bell. I could not remember if I had met Herr Jandl before, but I felt I must have done. I wasn't sure if we had met in 1997, but I knew he would know my name. He is a jovial white-haired man, an artist (mainly of local

The Villa Königsgarten

Landscapes, but comes across as slightly cold, although on the surface very welcoming. I feel there is something slightly enigmatic about him, so one never quite knows what he is thinking. This is a feeling I have come to be aware of in

Altaussee, the subtleties of which passed me by when I was younger – a feeling I would earlier have put down to a difference in language – but now I feel there is often a slight uncertainty lurking on their behalf, as to how I, an Englishman, whose family lost its home and livelihood in Austria, might now regard them. I often wonder if they feel I have come expecting some kind of forgiveness or restitution, rather than as an equal on friendly terms. But perhaps I am just imagining all this.

In any event, Herr Jandl answered the door and immediately knew who I was. He invited us in but he made some excuse as to why he couldn't spare a lot of time. He showed us round the ground floor, took us round the garden, and finally into his studio. We looked at his many half-finished paintings and made positive noises. But I listened to him with only one ear, as all the time I was trying to imagine how the house had looked in my grandfather's day, trying to imagine Ernst and my father living there, looking at the views they had from each of the windows, and imagining the influence these might have had on them.

Finally, before we left, Herr Jandl suddenly said we must come back in the morning, he had something to show me. I had no idea what it was. He said there was something in his attic he wanted to get down for me to see.

So, on the following morning, Sunday, we duly re-appeared at his house, and he led us to his studio. There, on an easel, was the plaque to Ernst. I could not have been more surprised. It bore the message I clearly remembered. In translation it reads:

'In memory of Ernst Königsgarten. He chose Altaussee as his last resting place yet died in Theresienstadt in 1942'

The meaning was clear to all. Theresienstadt was a concentration camp to which many Viennese Jews were sent. It was a stark reminder of Austria's Nazi past. I always felt my father must have been quite brave when he had the plaque made, but I had been brought up in the belief that Austria had been the first victim of Nazism rather than one of its collaborators. This was a view that not only suited post-war Austria, but one that also suited the Western Allies in 1945 as they sought to build a friendly bulwark in Eastern Europe against the newly-emerging Soviet Empire. The consequence of

The original plaque on an easel in Jandl's studio

this, which was no doubt unforeseen at the time, was that Austria took a lot longer to face up to its Nazi past than Germany – over 40 years longer in fact. It was not until questions arose in the late 1980s over Austrian President Waldheim's role during World War II that Austria was finally forced to face up to its complicity in the Nazi atrocities and to the fact that many ex-Nazis had been allowed to continue in their posts after the war. Only since then have serious attempts been made to right many of the wrongs committed in the Nazi era and to pay compensation to Nazi victims. My father must have been even braver than I had thought to have had the plaque made.

I was clearly surprised to see the plaque and I told Herr Jandl that I had noticed that the plaque was no longer in situ in the churchyard, and how glad I now was to see it was still in existence. He explained to me that when more space had been required in the churchyard old graves and plaques had been removed, and my grandfather's plaque had been put into the gardener's shed. When this in turn had required renovation, someone had passed the plaque to him, saying that as he lived in the Villa Königsgarten, perhaps he should look after it. The exact extent to which this explanation is true, and the willingness of Jandl to look after it, is something I will never know, but the story has a certain probability about it and the fact is that he had kept it safe and produced it now to show me.

I said straight away that I would like to see it re-instated in the churchyard and asked how I should go about this. He kindly said he would look after this for me, and that he would speak to the local priest and see if it could be done.

Over that winter (2010/11) I wrote several times to Herr Jandl to enquire about progress, and spoke to him on the telephone. He had told us in September that he had a heart condition and that he was due to have a by-pass operation later that autumn. So, firstly on that account, and then later with heavy winter snow on the ground (up to two metres in the village), there was always an excuse as to why the plaque had not yet been re-instated, but he was adamant that approval had been given and that it would be done. I did not mention money, but I was surprised that he did not mention it either (which of course increased my suspicion that it would not in fact be done). However I said that I was coming to Altaussee again in May and looked forward to seeing it restored by then.

So it was a surprise therefore when I spoke to Herr Jandl again in about April to be told that the snows had finally melted and that the plaque had indeed been re-instated. I said how grateful I was. I also confirmed that Bridget and I were coming out to Altaussee in May and I looked forward to seeing it back in its place.

* * *

The first time Bridget and I went to Altaussee in 2010 we had driven. We drove from her house near Queyssac-les-Vignes in France, spending the first night in a small hotel half-way up the Petit St. Bernard pass (where Hannibal might have crossed the Alps into Italy), with a magnificent view back down the valley into France. We then spent two nights in Bellagio on Lake Como, then drove via Switzerland and Germany to Berchtesgaden, where we spent another night, before descending down the mountains into Austria. Berchtesgaden is where Hitler had his mountain retreat, the Berghof, and also a grand 'tea-room' used for entertaining and known as the Eagle's Nest, built on the very summit of the mountain, with the most superb views in all directions. This had been built for him in 13 months in 1938 by slave labour, a present from Martin Bormann on the occasion of his fiftieth birthday, and is accessed by a polished brass art nouveau lift built deep inside the mountain. The Berghof is no longer in existence (all trace of it was removed after the war), but the Eagle's Nest certainly is, and is a popular tourist attraction. After leaving Berchtesgaden we stopped for lunch in the beautiful lakeside village of Hallstatt, before reaching Altaussee in the afternoon.

The ruins of the Berghof photographed by Henry in August 1945

This time, in May 2011, we flew to Munich, where we hired a car and drove directly to Altaussee. By the last post before we left home a letter arrived from Austria, with an Altaussee postmark. I did not recognize the handwriting nor know the sender. Her name was Ursula Kals-Friese and she explained that she had just seen the re-instated plaque to Ernst on the churchyard wall, that she had spoken to Herr Jandl, who had told her that it had been re-instated at my request, and that furthermore I was about to come out to Altaussee. She explained that she had been a secretary to the writer Friedrich Torberg who had lived in the Villa Königsgarten before Herr Jandl, and that she would very much like to meet me when we arrived. This turned out to be a significant moment in the whole of this great journey of discovery, one that would open up doors that I never knew existed. If that letter hadn't arrived when it did, none of the rest of this story might have happened.

I put the letter in my pocket, resolving to ring Ursula on our arrival, and we set off for the airport. We picked up our hire car in Munich, and joined the motorway heading east via Salzburg. In due course we turned off onto the familiar country roads which I knew from my youth, via Wolfgangsee – my father would always point out the White Horse Inn (*Der Weisse Rössl*) on the far side of the lake, made famous by a song – then Bad Ischl, where we stopped for a quick look round and a coffee and cream cake in *Zauner's* (again a rite of passage from my youth) before eventually driving up over the Pötschen Pass – a road which until after the war was almost impassable to motor traffic except in good conditions, and which had helped to keep the Aussee region more remote – and hence to Altaussee.

On this occasion we had decided not to stay at the *Seehotel*. It was sadly no longer the same as in my youth. The large old dining room and most of the bedrooms had gone – converted into self-contained holiday flats – and we had been attracted to the smaller *Gasthof Loser* when we had been lucky enough to eat there in September 2010 on the occasion of their last great waltz evening, with everyone in local costume, under the previous owner Herr Glaser.

Upon our arrival we immediately phoned Ursula and told her where we were staying. She was clearly not going to wait to meet us any longer than she had to, and said she would be at the hotel by the time we had finished our supper! She duly was. She is a dignified well-built woman, always dressed resplendently in a dirndl (a costume which suits all sizes!) and she speaks excellent English. We sat there over many glasses of wine, until they had to push us out well after eleven o'clock, and conversation never ceased. We told each other our life stories. Perhaps as a result of her work as Torberg's secretary, she had somehow become the central figure for all those with Jewish connections who had once had houses in Altaussee and who (or whose descendants) had now returned in one way or another. She was very knowledgeable and very well-read. Her husband Bruno, whom we subsequently met with her at her house, had a much more simple background. He had been a local salt miner and then mountain guide, but he played the accordion (his *Rumpel*) exceptionally well, and, unknown to us at the time, had been in the band at the last waltz evening we had been to at the *Gasthof Loser* in September 2010.

Ursula talked to us about the Villa Königsgarten, about its belongings, about an auction of its contents at the time of Miss Schiff's death in 1974, and about life in Altaussee then and now. But of course we also talked about the plaque. She described how she couldn't have been more surprised to suddenly see the plaque to Ernst re-instated, after so many years, but the reason why she had noticed it so easily was because it was now fixed on the outside of the churchyard wall, i.e. on the lakeside path itself, rather than on the inside, where she would of course have been less likely to see it. Had I requested this? she asked.

I said 'no', I had merely asked for it to be re-instated. We never really did discover why it had been affixed to the outside of the wall. Was it because we weren't paying any rent for it?

Was it because the churchyard wall was full? Or was it because they did not want a reminder of Nazi horrors inside the cemetery? We will probably never know. But when I offered (via Herr Jandl) to pay for its re-instatement, I was definitely told there would be no charge. Was there a certain communal guilt there too? Who knows?[3]

In any event, the re-instatement of the plaque had brought about our acquaintance with Ursula, and this in turn had several significant consequences.

The author with the re-instated plaque on the outside of the churchyard wall

First, it provided us with a link to the past. She had known the Villa Königsgarten one stage nearer to how it had been in Ernst's day. I now know that many items of Ernst's furniture were still in the house when Miss Schiff owned it. Ursula herself had bought three small items at the auction on Miss Schiff's death. One was a chandelier which she now had

---

[3] This plaque also mysteriously disappeared a few years later and I replaced it with a new one in 2018 (photo on p.iii of this book) which as of 2023 was still in place.

hanging in her house, and one was a mounted bas-relief Persian tile which she subsequently gave to Tessa and me, and which Tessa now has in her house in France.

Secondly, she understood a lot about Austria's role in past events, and was someone one could talk to about it (which was not generally the case).

Ursula and Bruno

And thirdly, she was responsible for our subsequent acquaintance with Carole Angier (about which more in due course).

The next day we went over to Ursula's house for tea. But it was not just tea. It was tea with champagne and specially made cakes, and we met her husband Bruno. We sat on the terrace in the sunshine, eating and drinking our champagne, while Bruno, in his lederhosen, played his *Rumpel*, including some of the music which we had loved so much from the waltz evening we had been to the autumn before.

We also visited the salt mine on that visit. As children, our parents had taken us to the salt mine on a couple of occasions, and I remember that on the first occasion there was definitely no official mention of the fact that the mine had been used to store works of art during the war. My father had however mentioned it to us somewhat secretly, in whispers, merely mentioning that the Nazis had hidden many prized paintings there and that the dry conditions created by the salt had helped to preserve them. He made no mention of the fact that many of these had been stolen from Jews or private owners or even that some of Ernst's collection had been stored there too. (As a child I would of course have been totally unaware of the extent to which the Nazis had plundered the museums and private collections of Western Europe.)

Even without this knowledge, which added a certain 'frisson' to any tour of the mine, the visit was not without its thrills. One had to put on a protective overall and carry a Hurricane lamp, one walked along a good mile or two of tunnels, one descended slopes down polished wooden slides, and one passed through huge caverns, one with a lake with an island in the middle, all beautifully lit, where concerts were given from time to time; so the tour was of sufficient interest in itself even without any public admission having to be made about its more sinister past. But as the years went by the Austrians became more open about their history and mention began to be made of the storage of artworks. Now, if you visit the mine, as I did again in 2012, much is made of this aspect of its history. You are even shown a sample of some of the racks where the paintings were stored, and you are shown a short film. You see photos of the paintings arriving by the lorry-load during the war, and then photos of the Resistance and the Americans recovering them at the end of the war.

But, they are still not entirely honest. The 'official' explanation given by the guide in 2012 was that the paintings had come mainly from the museums of Austria, and that they were stored there for their protection from the bombing, and not that they included many artworks seized from private Jewish collections or foreign museums or churches, secretly concealed, and intended for Hitler's proposed new museum in Linz.

In any event the fact that stolen works of art had been hidden there during the war had caught my imagination from my earliest childhood visit, and when I saw a book on the subject in about 2004 in a London bookshop, I bought it. It was called *The Lost Masters*, by two Englishmen, Peter Harclerode and Brendan Pittaway. It tells the full story, in all its incredible detail, of how Hitler had planned well before the outbreak of war to seize major works of art from across Europe and have them installed in his proposed new *Hitlermuseum* being designed for him by his architect Albert Speer and which was to be built in grand classical style in Linz. This was to become the new cultural centre of Europe to replace Paris and Vienna, where as a failed art student Hitler had felt snubbed and rejected. (There is a well-known photograph taken during the war of Hitler standing beside Albert Speer poring over a model of this new centre of Linz.) The fact is that in the years leading up to the war, Hitler had sent out secret agents to all the major museums and art collections of Western Europe to identify and catalogue all their contents, and a list was drawn up of the major items to be seized once he was in power and able to do so. The premeditated aspect of this plunder is, rather surprisingly, little known.

The book was fascinating. It also describes the true story, which was made into a film in the 1960s with Burt Lancaster, called *The Train*, in which the French Resistance successfully prevented the last trainload of paintings from leaving France, re-routing the train onto a circular route which ended up back in Paris, by re-naming all the stations it passed through with the names of the stations it should have passed through on its way to Germany!

Another section of the book describes the role played by the Altaussee salt miners and local Freedom Fighters. Led by a local man from Bad Aussee called Albrecht Gaiswinkler, who had made his way to England and was then dropped in the area by parachute by the RAF in the last months of the war, they succeeded in preventing the Nazis from carrying out Hitler's so-called 'Nero Order' to blow up the mine with all the paintings in it. They removed the giant bomb placed inside the mine by the Nazis and blew up the mine entrance with detonators, so as to block it and prevent the bomb being reinstated, thus securing it until the arrival of the Americans on 10 May (two days after the war ended).

Although the extent of the role played by Gaiswinkler is played down in the second book (an American publication) I read on the subject, *The Monuments Men* by Robert Edsel (recently made into a rather second-rate film by George Clooney), the name Albrecht Gaiswinkler stayed in my mind as having been a key and significant player in this drama.

Over Christmas and the New Year 2010/2011, when Tessa and I were clearing out our mother's house in Sulgrave, we went through all her books and boxed them up. However these also included many books of our father's which had not really been looked at in any detail since he died in 1988. So I couldn't believe my eyes when I suddenly came across the name Albrecht Gaiswinkler on the spine of a book, called *Sprung in die Freiheit* (A Jump to Freedom). I was even more surprised when I saw a handwritten dedication by Gaiswinkler to my father, dated 1 August 1949, inside the book. Clearly my father had met Gaiswinkler when he was in Altaussee at that time. Although he had by then recovered Ernst's house and sold it to Miss Schiff, I have since discovered he was still trying to recover some of Ernst's furniture and works of art. Some had even been stored for safe-keeping by the Nazis in four crates in the salt mine. He would almost certainly have met Gaiswinkler as part of that process - Gaiswinkler was by then a local Councillor. But what intrigued me most was that my father had never mentioned Gaiswinkler to us, not even when he took us to the salt mine in those first visits to Altaussee. The story of Gaiswinkler being dropped by parachute to lead a team of local Resistance fighters to save Europe's greatest works of art is a thrilling tale of derring-do and it is very strange that my father never mentioned it to us once, even though he had met him and couldn't fail to have known the story. But of course that might have led to him getting drawn into discussing other events which he had clearly decided to put behind him. All very sad.

Through his book I gathered that Gaiswinkler had been born and grew up in Bad Aussee. As an ardent anti-Nazi he joined the local Resistance, but then in 1943, to avoid the growing attention of the authorities, he enlisted in the Luftwaffe. He was posted first to Belgium and then to France. In April 1944 he defected and managed to cross the lines and join the French Resistance. Then in September of that year he surrendered to the advancing Americans and told them of the artworks concealed in the Altaussee salt mine. The British were quick to take him up on this and he was taken to England and trained as a double agent. Then in February 1945 he was dropped by parachute, along with three others, into the snow-covered mountains around Altaussee with the aim of rallying the local partisans and, amongst other objectives, saving the hidden artworks from destruction. Even if he exaggerates his role in his book (as was later alleged), he was undoubtedly a significant player in that whole drama, and it was thrilling to think that my father had met him.

By the time I had finished Gaiswinkler's book, (I retreated to bed with it and a dictionary for many weeks), I had begun to realise that there were a number of stories which my father could have told us, but had not done so. How many more were there? Clearly more research was required.

Before Bridget and I left Altaussee in 2011 we looked out Gaiswinkler's old house, situated in a pretty meadow above Bad Aussee. We also sought out the Villa Kerry high above Altaussee, which had become the headquarters of the SS in the last days of the war. Both houses featured largely in Gaiswinkler's book. It seemed hard to imagine the frightening events which had once taken place in those two idyllic locations.

* * *

Once back home I phoned my cousin Thea in Vancouver to tell her of my trip and find out what more I could. Thea told me she had spent many summers in Altaussee at the same time as my father. Like many others, her parents had rented the same house there every year. She even sent me a photograph of her father, my father, her mother and herself all in their swimming costumes by the lake taken in 1930. She was eleven years younger than my father and he was often deputed to chaperone her when she was invited out by young men! From the 1930 photograph alone (when she was only 12), one can tell she would later have attracted many admirers.

In June 1937 she married Robert Bloch-Bauer and a year later gave birth to her first son, George. As Robert was not only Ferdinand Bloch-Bauer's nephew but also his personal assistant, they not only lived close to him in Vienna, but in early summer 1938 they joined Ferdinand (Adele having died of meningitis in 1925) at his castle *Schloss Jungfern* (now *Panenske-Brezany*) near Prague in Czechoslovakia. Thea told me it was very grand, but it didn't have a swimming pool! The summer was very hot and she was pregnant!

Notwithstanding the lack of a swimming pool, it must have been one of the more impressive houses near Prague, because after the Nazi occupation of the country the castle was seized and occupied by Reinhard Heydrich. Heydrich was one of the authors of Hitler's 'Final Solution' (the extermination of the Jews) and in September 1941 was appointed the so-called *Reichsprotektor* of Bohemia and Moravia in place of the previous incumbent who was considered 'too soft' on the Czechs. Heydrich used the Bloch-Bauer castle as his residence until he was assassinated in May 1942. During that time he, and the *Einsatzgruppen* which he controlled, ruthlessly suppressed Czech culture and deported or executed any members of the Czech resistance who were captured. A similar fate applied to the Jews. His aim was to create a German region which after the war would be incorporated directly into the German Reich. Brutal reprisals, however, followed his assassination. Over 13,000 people were arrested, deported or imprisoned, and over 1,300 were massacred in villages falsely linked to the assassins. (Hitler's original orders had been even worse, but he had been persuaded to temper his response as Germany needed the Czech workforce.) But this all happened, of course, well after the Bloch-Bauers had left. I visited the castle (more a manor house really) in 2021, where a detailed account of the assassination and its aftermath is displayed in the garden.

Panenske-Brezany (in 2021)

In the autumn of 1938 Thea and Robert returned to Vienna. But Hitler had annexed Austria in March of that year and had immediately introduced a whole raft of anti-Jewish legislation. Family paintings and jewellery were seized from the Bloch-Bauers by the Nazis as they stood by and watched (one ring ended up on the hand of Göring's wife) and by the autumn life had become very uncomfortable. But however uncomfortable it was, it seems that my father was more alarmed than they were, because Thea remembers him coming out to Vienna (from London) to persuade them to leave. He said things were much worse than they seemed to realise. Perhaps the arrival of his mother (Lisi) in London at the beginning of September, with stories of life in Vienna and Berlin, had alerted my father to the dangers that Thea and her family were facing. (This must have been quite a brave move on my father's part, since he hadn't secured permanent residence in England at that time and he still had a Czech passport.)

Thea in 1955

What happened next was a remarkable escape story, worthy of any thriller movie. On 20 October 1938 Thea, Robert, and their young son George (born on 16 June 1938) managed to escape by train into Hungary, and from there into Yugoslavia, where they were kept hidden for six weeks in the small stationmaster's house at the end of a private railway line leading to a quarry owned by the Bloch-Bauer family.

Thanks to the help of a number of intermediaries, and some considerable bribes, they were then driven to the middle of a field one dark night, where it had been arranged that the Orient Express from Belgrade would stop and take them on board. That Ferdinand Bloch-Bauer was a director of the Oriental Railway Company which had built part of the line, may have helped a bit too. In any event, the lights of the train eventually hove into sight, and despite their fears that it would not stop, notwithstanding the bribes, it did so. One single door opened and steps were put down, they ran across the field towards the lighted doorway, and with baby George in Thea's arms they climbed aboard. The door closed behind them and they found themselves in a sealed carriage crossing Central Europe towards the English Channel and safety.

Once in England they got papers to emigrate to Canada and embarked by boat for Halifax, Nova Scotia on 24 December. They then had a five-day train journey across Canada in sub-zero temperatures, during which baby George was taken ill, but they eventually all arrived safely in Vancouver on 7 January 1939. Thea is still living there now, a grand matriarch with many grandchildren and great-grandchildren. But there is one surprising sequel to her escape story: she managed to get her furniture out too. Somehow she got an export permit and the furniture was shipped during the summer of 1939 from Hamburg to Vancouver via the Panama Canal. But as the German ship was returning to Germany, war was declared and the ship was torpedoed. So the furniture only just made it! She still has it in her house to this day.

Thea's widowed mother, Ada, followed her to Vancouver from Vienna by an equally unorthodox route. Two gay Dutchmen who were living in Vienna arranged two false marriages to Ada and a friend, as a result of which Ada and her friend were able to acquire Dutch passports and exit visas to Holland, in return for which Ada and her friend paid for hospital treatment in Vienna needed by one of the Dutchmen. This is how Ada, whom I knew in my youth, acquired the Dutch surname Jongman, which she continued to use for the rest of her life, even though she never saw the Dutchman again. (This was another story which I only discovered all these years later, from Thea, and not from my parents.)

Thea (centre) in Altaussee in the 1970s with two granddaughters and the author's parents Jean (L) and Henry (R)

I now had a picture that began to make sense. It was quite clear that the Jewish connection with my family was not a remote connection 'some way back in the past' but, as far as the Nazis were concerned anyway, very much more real and recent.

The author with Thea in Vancouver on the occasion of her 100th birthday – 30th March 2018

Chapter Three: The National Archives

As previously mentioned, I had begun to build up the family tree on Geni. However, I was not the only person researching my family history. In early 2013 a cousin I had not heard of before, John Fisher, who lives mainly in Northern Ireland, had seen the entries I had completed on Geni and contacted me asking about Max Bohne. Max was the second husband of my grandmother Lisi. I had known of Max's name since childhood, as Lisi's surname during my lifetime was in fact Bohne, but we had been told very little about him apart from the fact that he came from Berlin. If we ever asked what had become of him, we had merely been told that he had died. We knew that Lisi had gone to live in Berlin, but when and for how long we did not know. Furthermore, we assumed that Max had died some time before Lisi came to England, as we knew she had been living in Vienna immediately prior to the war. We assumed therefore that she had been widowed a second time sometime prior to 1938 (and incidentally so did my Aunt Anne, Hugo's wife, until I advised her otherwise quite recently).

John Fisher told me that Max had died in Theresienstadt. I said that he must be mistaken – there must perhaps be two Max Bohnes or he had somehow muddled him up with Ernst. I could not believe they had both died in Theresienstadt, or that if so, my father had remained so quiet about the fate of Max. It also meant that when Lisi came to England in 1938 she would not have been a widow after all, but still married. How and why did she leave him? Or how and why did she escape and not him?

I checked the Holocaust records online and yes, a Max Bohne had indeed died in Theresienstadt on 23 July 1943. From further information I was able to obtain, it became clear that this was indeed Lisi's second husband. The picture became bleaker by the minute. My grandmother Lisi had had an even more tragic life than I had realised.

Clearly more research was required and at about this time I had the idea of contacting the National Archives for my father's and Lisi's naturalization records. I thought they would at least confirm the respective dates of their arrival in the UK and possibly details of Lisi's marriage to Max. Little did I know they would reveal much more.

The National Archives are now housed in a purpose-built modern building near Kew Gardens, but many records are available online. I soon found a record of Lisi's, Hugo's and my father's Naturalization Certificates. Although I was able to access a copy of their Certificates online, I also discovered there were related files dealing with the applications which can only be viewed in person. These are normally kept closed for 100 years but can be released (in a redacted form if necessary) following a Freedom of Information Act request. I set about putting such requests in hand. It takes about six weeks for a request to be answered, but they were all successful and I was eventually advised that the files had been released. I then needed to make arrangements to visit the National Archives and view the files on site. And so several weeks later, in July 2013, I set out. I ascertained that one could take photographs of the files, so I took my camera with me.

I felt very excited by the trip. I took the Underground to Kew Gardens on a fine summer day and walked through leafy suburban streets following signs to the National Archives. On one's first visit one has to register. This involves having one's photograph taken, one's passport photocopied, and ultimately being issued with a Reader's Card. You can then request the files that you require.

The files duly appeared – a rather fat one for my father, and rather thinner ones for Lisi and Hugo. Here suddenly was an insight, albeit a small one, but still an insight, into parts of their lives about which I knew nothing. What I felt sad about was that there was really no obvious reason why my father had never been more forthcoming with more details of his past, or those of his mother and brother. But equally Tessa and I had never seen fit to quiz him. It is hard to diagnose to what extent this was due to a lack of inquisitiveness on our part or to what extent it was because we felt this was a taboo subject. Tessa and I have discussed this since, and we are both agreed that it was not just a lack of interest on our behalf which was responsible for our ignorance.

Henry's file

My father's file begins with a letter dated 5 August 1937 from his solicitors Herbert Smith to the Under Secretary of State at the Home Office (Aliens Department), begging to apply for permission for my father to return to this country on or before 15 September and permanently to reside here. My father is described as 'Dr. Henry Koenigsgarten of Bratislava, Czechoslovakia'.

The letter then continues by giving a brief outline of the relevant background to his application, the salient points of which were considered to be the following, namely that:-

(i) My father was born in Brno in 1907 'of a highly respectable and wealthy family of industrialists'. His father was named as 'Mr. Friedrich Königsgarten';

(ii) He was 'brought up in Brno and Vienna and finished his public school education in Berlin';

(iii) He then worked as a 'volunteer' with a firm of bankers while at the same time studying law at the universities of Berlin and then Leipzig, where in 1929 he qualified as a 'Doctor of Law summa cum laude';

(iv) He came to London at the end of 1929 where until 1931 'he perfected his knowledge of English' and studied English law, as well as obtaining experience in banking with a firm of merchant bankers, Leopold Joseph & Sons;

(v) In 1931 'while on a trip to the Continent' he was offered a position as a Managing Director of a French banking business in Paris called Comptoir-Franco-Danubien. This he accepted and remained there until 1936 becoming the Head of Foreign Exchange and Securities;

(vi) In 1936 he resigned his position with the bank as he disapproved of the way its new Dutch owners handled the business, and accepted a position with the Syndicate of the Slovakian Sugar Industry in Bratislava.

Henry on his motorbike in Altaussee

The letter finished by explaining that Dr Koenigsgarten had been approached by Messrs. Hart, Son & Co., Merchant Bankers in London, with a view to his 'gradually taking over the management of their foreign business', and ultimately

Henry (second from right) in Juan-les-Pins 1931

becoming a partner in the firm. One of the few details of my father's career that he had passed on to me personally was that this offer had been made to him by the Senior Partner of Hart Son & Co. who had met him while on holiday in Bratislava – something my father had not expected when he took up the job in what he rather regarded as the back of beyond!

A conditional six-month permit was granted and on 28 October 1937 my father landed at Newhaven 'on the early boat' (to quote the Immigration Officer's Report).

Six months later Hart Son & Co. wrote to the Home Office, applying to extend the permit, expressing considerable satisfaction with my father's ability to develop the business, crediting him with the fact that the bank had not had to lay off any staff during the recent 'serious recession' brought about by 'political crises both at home and abroad'.

A six-month extension was granted, namely until 28 October 1938.

On 11 October 1938 Hart Son & Co. wrote to extend the permit once again, this time giving details of the additional business my father had brought to the firm, and also confirming that he had now been offered a partnership.

On 14 December 1938 the Home Office finally removed any time restriction on my father's stay in the UK, but for the time being he was only permitted to 'engage in business as Partner with Hart Son & Co'. Any other employment or business had to be authorised by the Secretary of State and my father was reminded that 'the stay of every foreigner in the United Kingdom is conditional on good behaviour and the Secretary of State reserves to himself the power to require any foreigner to leave the country at any time'. (Our immigration problems might be relieved at a stroke if the Secretary of State were to exercise such powers today!)

Just prior to this letter confirming that there was no longer any time restriction to my father's stay in the United Kingdom is an interesting little document in the file. It is a 'Copy of Card in Traffic Index' for Arrivals at the Port of Dover on 30 November 1938. It shows that my father arrived that day from Dunkirk. I do not know where he had been, but the removal of the time restriction on his stay in the UK had not yet been confirmed (there is a note to that effect on the Arrival Card) so his re-entry into the UK could have been fraught with difficulty. It must have been a worrying moment.

The next letter in the file is again from Herbert Smith, dated 30 December 1938, this time requesting permission for my father to change the spelling of his surname. They explain that 'he has the greatest difficulty in making his name understood and having it pronounced and spelt correctly when written in one word'. The need for such permission was due to the Aliens Restriction (Amendment) Act 1919 as a result of which any change of name by an 'alien' was restricted. Permission was sought to write his name as Koenigs-Garten. It might be thought that such a minor change was not worth seeking, but I imagine it was felt that anything more might be refused and that once he was allowed to write his name in two words, albeit hyphenated, who was to stop anyone just using one of the words for convenience? It took the Home Office nearly three months to reply, but by letter dated 14 March 1939 permission was granted.

From October 1937 to September 1939 my father is stated as living at 140 Piccadilly. He often spoke of living in a service flat in Hamilton Place, and indeed the entrance to 140 Piccadilly is indeed in Hamilton Place. This is at the bottom of Park Lane, just behind the InterContinental Hotel. In any event, he often mentioned that he would never have ventured out into Piccadilly in those days at night without being in full evening dress! How times have changed!

In September 1939 he moved to 43 Hays Mews, just off Berkeley Square, no doubt an equally prestigious address.

In April 1940 a new firm of solicitors, Joynson-Hicks & Co., wrote to the Home Office on his behalf (spelling his name in the heading as Henry Koenigs Garten, but referring to him in the letter simply as Mr. Garten) stating that their client had been trying to obtain permission from the War Office 'to join the British Army'. Apparently approval had first to be obtained from the Tribunal dealing with Czechoslovakian Refugees, and it was not known what stage his application had reached. This time a more speedy response was obtained and by letter dated 18 April 1940 the Home Office confirmed that Mr. Henry Koenigs Garten had been 'passed as a friendly alien'.

The way was now open for my father to join the British Army which he duly did in June 1940. At that stage however, all 'aliens' were obliged to join what was called the Pioneer Corps and were, seemingly, kept well away from active service. In my father's case, he was sent to remote parts of the British Isles to build camps for prisoners of war, including one for Italians in Scotland, 'because he was known to be good at languages'. But Italian was in fact one language he did not speak!

Henry in wartime uniform

By December 1942 he was recommended for a commission by his Commanding Officer and had done an appropriate training course. But he was keen to serve in a fighting unit, and such a transfer would be made easier were he to be granted British nationality. On 14 December 1942 he therefore completed his first application for naturalization, which was submitted on his behalf by Herbert Smith on 21 December with a request that the application be treated as a special case to enable him to transfer to a fighting unit.

Once again the Home Office took their time to reply before advising Herbert Smith on 30 April 1943 that all naturalization applications had been 'suspended generally'. It is perhaps worth noting that in his application for naturalization my father had given the following information:-

(i) that his father's full name was 'Bedrich Koenigsgarten'. This is interesting as it would indicate that at some stage before his death (in 1927) Fritz/Friedrich adopted the Czech form of his Christian name, or maybe my father just wanted to emphasize his Czech nationality; although in the next line he states that at the time of his death his father's nationality was 'Austro-Hungarian';

(ii) that his mother Elisabeth ('Lisi') Koenigsgarten, née Brück, was 'stateless', but of Austro-Hungarian origin. She was at this time living in Woodstock Road, Oxford;

(iii) that he himself had acquired Czechoslovakian nationality 'by virtue of the constitution of the Czechoslovakian Republic'; and

(iv) that since October 1937 he had spent 12 days in France, 8 days in Czechoslovakia, 3 days in Switzerland and 3 days in Austria.

In July 1943 there is a note in the file that the 'Army Council, in conjunction with the civil authorities have authorised' my father to change his name from 'Henry Koenigs-Garten' to 'Henry Kenneth Garton'.

On 4 October 1944 Herbert Smith were again sent in to bat against the Home Office. It was pointed out that my father had now been granted a Commission and his rank was Second Lieutenant, and that furthermore he was about to marry my mother 'Miss Jean McRae, a British Subject, daughter of Colonel H. St. G. M. McRae, O.B.E., D.S.O. &c. of Budleigh Salterton, Devon, and a V.A.D. Nurse in the Red Cross since the outbreak of war'. Herbert Smith went on to say that Miss McRae was 'particularly desirous to retain her British nationality and not to acquire Czech nationality on her marriage to Mr. Garton'.

The Home Office replied rather pompously and stuffily on 17 October to say that 'if, as the Secretary of State understands is the case, a woman of British nationality would in Czechoslovakian law acquire Czechoslovakian nationality on marriage to a Czechoslovakian subject, she would thereupon be deemed in British law to have lost British nationality'. The Home Office went on to say that as regards my father's application for naturalization, the position remained as stated in their letter of 30 April 1943.

*Henry and Jean's wedding
(Hugo extreme left, Lisi extreme right)*

Notwithstanding the above, my parents got married on 16 November 1944 while both were on leave, in the church at Budleigh Salterton, my maternal grandparents' home. As with most wartime weddings it was perforce a very small affair, but the photographs show the presence not only of my mother's parents, but also my father's mother Lisi and his brother Hugo.

My parents had met at an 'Other Ranks' Dance in Romsey Town Hall some time before he was commissioned. My father had been stationed at that time in Southampton and my mother at Netley near Romsey. The men and the women were sitting on opposite sides of the Hall and he had walked over and asked her to dance. (The previous soldier to walk over had merely wanted to open the window!) Their relationship obviously flourished and eventually my maternal grandmother took a train from Budleigh Salterton to Southampton to check him out (yes, the pun was often repeated!). There was some reference to a 'charming Czech' and my grandparents gave their approval.

On her marriage my mother automatically acquired Czech nationality. She retained her British passport but her nationality was changed to Czech.

In December 1943, my father had succeeded in transferring from the Pioneer Corps to the West Yorkshire Infantry Regiment. He was commissioned in August 1944 and in March 1945 was posted to No.4 Information Control Unit stationed in Hamburg. This was a unit whose role was (in my father's words) 'to try and re-establish normal life in Germany after the war'. This involved publishing a local newspaper and re-opening cinemas and the like. Inevitably it proved to be the most interesting period of his wartime career, particularly the last few weeks of the war and the first few weeks of peace. Germany surrendered on 8 May 1945, and on 10 May my father was sent to take over the last remaining German radio station. This was broadcasting from Flensburg on the Baltic Coast, where Admiral Dönitz (nominated by Hitler as his successor) had set up his headquarters after Hitler's suicide on 30 April. As a result my father found himself involved in negotiating the transitional arrangements whereby German soldiers had to lay down their arms and return to peace-time activities. He was the first British soldier to arrive in Flensburg after Germany's surrender, having had to drive past thousands of still-armed German soldiers and through a number of roadblocks (which he told his driver not to stop at) to get there. He was then driven in Dönitz's open Mercedes (which had previously belonged to Hitler until his suicide) to Dönitz's headquarters, where he agreed the instructions to be broadcast over the radio. He narrowly missed meeting Admiral Dönitz himself. A letter he wrote to my mother the following day describing the events of that visit is reproduced in Appendix III of this book. He continued to be involved in the Flensburg hand-over arrangements until they were concluded.

Henry's photos of the 'Flensburg Incident'
10–13 May 1945

There is one further anecdote my father told us about his time in Hamburg. In August he was sent with a Canadian driver to Munich to collect the well-known German opera singer Hans Hotter. The idea was for Hotter to sing in Hamburg as part of a plan to get some kind of entertainment reinstated for the inhabitants. As it was not too much of a detour, my father got the driver to go via Salzburg and Altaussee. While my father visited a few of the sights of Salzburg, he recalled that the driver merely sat in the car! (Ten years later my cousin Thea found herself sitting next to this driver on a Greyhound bus in Canada!) In Altaussee my father made his first post-war visit to Ernst's house, and from the office of the local authority he obtained a formal letter confirming his ownership of the property as Ernst's legal successor.

But back in Hamburg his military work was still being hampered by the question of his nationality. On 3 July 1945 his Commanding Officer had written a memo stating that 'in view of the nature of his work with Information Control, it is most desirable that Capt. Garton become a British subject as soon as possible'. This was forwarded by Herbert Smith to the Home Office under cover of a letter dated 30 July in which they reiterated my father's request for naturalization.

Newspaper cutting of Admiral Dönitz leaving his headquarters on 15 May 1945

Once again the Home Office took their time to reply (although on this occasion they at least stated that 'the delay in replying' was 'regretted') but on 19 September 1945 they advised that the policy on naturalization had not changed.

Meanwhile my mother and her VAD unit had followed the advancing Allies as they moved across Europe. She was initially posted to Belgium, but in August 1945 she too was posted to Hamburg. Husbands and wives were not meant to be stationed in the same place, but they kept quiet and no one complained.

The queue for Information Control's German language newspaper

My mother recalled arriving in Hamburg on VJ Day (15 August) – the day the Japanese surrendered – as there were blackboards announcing the event on the stations they passed through. When they arrived in Hamburg they had to disembark outside the station, as it had been so badly bombed it was still unusable. They took over a civilian hospital on the outskirts of the city which was still intact, and my mother often recalled the queues of Germans who could be seen picking through the hospital dustbins every morning, such was the shortage of food. The centre of Hamburg was still nothing but rubble, even though the war in Europe had by then been over for more than three months.

Hamburg July 1945 (photographed by Henry)

In October 1945 my father was 'de-mobbed' and returned to civilian life in London. My mother wasn't de-mobbed until January 1946, but as my parents had kept quiet about both being stationed in Hamburg, his colleagues envied him as they thought he would be returning home to his wife. He pointed out, to their surprise, that actually he was leaving her behind in Hamburg!

My father took up residence in 25 Tufton Court, SW1, in a flat owned by my mother's aunt Eva Bell, and resumed his career with Hart Son & Co. On 20 March 1946 he renewed his application for naturalization, this time on a special form 'for Aliens who have served in His Majesty's Forces and been discharged'. But the application was still not without its hurdles. On 4 June there is a mysterious note to the effect that 'in 1938 we were informed of a suspicion that Koenigsgarten was involved in espionage'. The name of the informant has been redacted and will remain closed until 2047! However, it goes on to state: 'Nothing has come to our notice which in any way confirms this suspicion' and that there are no further 'unfavourable reports' from the point of view of security. That may have been one hurdle. The next was how to divest himself of his Czech nationality.

There is a reference to a letter of 31 July from the Home Office (but the copy is missing from the file) stating that they would be prepared to grant a certificate of naturalization on production of evidence that my father had either already lost or would lose his Czech citizenship upon such an event. My father took up the matter with the Czech authorities in London.

The Czechoslovak Consulate General in Grosvenor Place, SW1, issued a document under seal on 19 October 1946 advising that my father's application for release from his Czech citizenship had been submitted to the appropriate authorities in Czechoslovakia, but that they were unable to state how long it would take for a certificate to be issued. They went on to say that it was quite possible that a reply would never be forthcoming, and it was also possible that my father's Czech nationality had already been lost since he had not been resident in Czechoslovakia for twenty years and had not renewed his Czech passport since it had expired in 1942. My father wrote to the Home Office to that effect, and finally on 16 December 1946 a Certificate of Naturalization was issued. The file concludes there. He was finally a British citizen. My mother too therefore regained her British nationality at the same time.

Three months later I was born. My parents were by then living in 41 Hasker Street, SW3, a small house in Chelsea which they had bought. (Chelsea was not so expensive in those days!) In 1949, when I was two, they moved 'round the corner' to 8 Moore Street, where they remained for the rest of my childhood.

Lisi's file

Lisi's file was much slimmer, but it still revealed facts about her which I had not known, particularly her connection with Oxford. It begins with a Certificate of Identity issued to her on 22 March 1939. It states:

'The present certificate is issued for the sole purpose of providing the holder with identity papers in lieu of a national passport. It is without prejudice to and in no way affects the national status of the holder. If the holder obtains a national passport it ceases to be valid and must be surrendered to the issuing authority.'

It gives her surname as Bohne-Koenigsgarten, her forename as Elise and her date of birth as 7 August 1884. (She understates her age! She was actually born in 1881.) It gives her nationality of origin as Austrian, her birthplace as 'Brun (Brno)' and her former residence abroad as Vienna. Her present address is given as 32 Craven Hill Gardens, London, W2.

The next item in the file is her Application for Naturalization dated 20 July 1947. This time she correctly states her age. By this date she was living in 2A Crick Road, Oxford, but her previous addresses are given with their relevant dates. She moved to Oxford (2 Park Town – she seems to have forgotten Bardwell Road) in August 1939, to 111 Woodstock Road in January 1942 and then to Crick Road in October 1945. She gives the details of her two marriages, namely to Fritz Koenigsgarten on 5 April 1903 in Brno, and to Max Bohne on 1 April 1915 in Berlin. She states that she acquired German nationality by virtue of her second marriage, and she gives the dates and places of death of both husbands, namely 18 January 1908 in Brno, and in Max's case 'Tereczin', stating merely '1942'. Details are provided of four referees who sign and attest to their knowledge of Lisi, and vouch for her 'good character and loyalty'. Finally the application is witnessed by a Commissioner of Oaths.

There follows a three-page report by the Oxford City Police. This reiterates and confirms the details given above and states that 'she is of good character, and has an adequate knowledge of the English language'. It states that she is financially solvent and that her income consists of '£150 per annum allowed her by her younger son, Henry Kenneth Garton......and the interest on £2,000 of various shares which she owns'. It advises that she 'owns the furniture of the 5-roomed flat which she shares with her brother and sister-in-law, Mr. and Mrs. Ernest Bruck. Her share of the rent of the flat amounts to £16 per quarter'. Finally, it gives details of her two sons, Hugo and Henry, and the various referees.

The application was successful and on 16 February 1948 Lisi was granted a Certificate of Naturalization. Finally, to complete the process, on 18 February 1948 she was required to swear an Oath of Allegiance 'to King George the Sixth, His Heirs and Successors, according to law'.

Henry and Lisi photographed in local costume

Hugo's file

Hugo's file is equally slim but nevertheless not without interest. It begins with his initial Application for Naturalization dated 29 April 1943. He gives his address as 'New College, Oxford' and his occupation as 'schoolmaster and writer'. He gives his date of birth as 13 April 1904 and, most interestingly for me, his place of birth as 'Dornych, Brno (Czechoslovakia)'. This was the family house adjoining his father's factory which I subsequently managed to track down and visit in 2014 – see later in this account - and where I presume my father was also born. Once again, I am surprised how I could have been so ignorant of these details until about 25 years after my father's death!

Hugo (left) and Henry (right) in Vienna 1914

Continuing with the Application, Hugo gives his 'father's full name in his country of origin' as 'Bedrich Koenigsgarten', Bedrich being the Czech form of Frederick (for which Fritz was the shortened form), but he quite correctly states his father's nationality at the time of his death as 'Austro-Hungarian'. He gives his own nationality as 'Czechoslovakian' by virtue of 'the constitution of the Czechoslovakian Republic in 1918'.

He goes on to give the addresses in London at which he lived from the date of his arrival in March 1938 until September 1939. During this time he was not permitted to take up employment, that being one of the conditions of his entry into the UK, but this was then varied to allow him to take up a position in September 1939 as a teacher at Cranemoor School, Highcliffe-on-Sea, Hants. He remained there until August 1940. In a 1929 directory of Schools and Tutors, Cranemoor is described as *'a coaching establishment on new lines'*. It goes on to state:

'...... Much outdoor life. Generous well-balanced diet, with abundant vitamins, wholemeal bread and new milk. A marked improvement in general physique is observed in boys commencing residence at Cranemoor. Fourteen acres of playing fields and paddocks. Electric lighting and modern sanitation.' (Thank God for that!)

Hugo was not an outdoors person. He must have struggled there! However there are a couple of amusing stories attached to his time there. In the opening years of the war, due to the fear of invasion, no foreigners were allowed within five miles of the coast, but the school was very much on the coast. So he was permitted to stay there provided he reported to the Police Station every week. But the Police Station was two miles away and he didn't have a bicycle. However the local policeman did have one, so to solve the problem it was agreed that the policeman would bicycle every week to the school to check he was still there, and everyone was satisfied! What a world!

The other anecdote concerns the air-raid practices that each member of staff was obliged to conduct with the boys.

There was one busybody of a female teacher who was quite convinced that because of his guttural German accent, Hugo must be a German spy and maintained that he was signalling to the German planes with his torch as he was leading the boys to the air-raid shelter! The fact that he had fled Austria on the arrival of the Nazis seems to have escaped her!

Not surprisingly this post did not fulfil his musical and literary ambitions, and evidence of this can be found in a letter I have come across dated July 1940 from Hugo to Fritz Reiner in Westport, Connecticut seeking his assistance in getting an immigration visa to America. Reiner was a prominent Hungarian conductor who had emigrated to America in 1922, but who also happened to be a second cousin of Hugo's whom he had known well in earlier times. But America was clamping down on immigrants and Reiner was unable to assist.

Fortunately in September 1940 Hugo obtained a teaching position at New College School in Oxford. Although this was another boys' prep school and therefore once again unlikely to have satisfied Hugo intellectually, he was at least now in Oxford, not only a more intellectual environment and one where he felt at home, but also where his mother was living.

Having now resigned himself to living in England, he applied for British naturalization. However, his first application came to nothing, for the same reason as my father's – all applications having been suspended during the war. In September 1945 he moved to St Edward's School, Oxford, and while he was there he made a second application in March 1946. This one was accompanied by (take a deep breath) a 'Statement in support of a claim for priority of consideration for an application for naturalization submitted by an alien engaged in one of the professions, or in business on his own account, or who is otherwise self-employed, and who considers that he has made during the war, or is now in a position to make, a substantial contribution to the interests of the country'! Hugo gave brief details of his 'full time teaching throughout the war' and his 'contribution to foreign broadcasts (Germany)'. He set out his reasons as to why he considered his application for naturalization to be deserving of priority as follows:

'In my career as a teacher at Public Schools and University Lecturer, British Nationality would be a great asset to me. I also hope to contribute to the re-education in Germany, through BBC, etc.'

His application took a while to process. In January 1947 he got a position as a teacher at Westminster School in London, where he taught French, German, Latin and History, and moved to 12 Queen's Gate Gardens, SW7. In May 1947 the Metropolitan Police, Special Branch, produced a report which contained nothing adverse. It gave details of e.g. his career, his earnings and his bank account, and stated that he 'appears to lead a quiet life and to live within his means'. Interestingly enough it states 'Although he is of Jewish origin, he became a member of the Church of England soon after he came to this country'. It also confirms that Hugo had written three scripts for the BBC overseas service in the previous few years.

There is one amusing entry which states that he came to the attention of the Special Branch in 1945 when he 'gave lectures on German poetry and kindred subjects to members of the Free German League of Culture, a communist inspired organisation.' Fortunately for his application it goes on to state: 'Questioned on this point, applicant said he had never been a member of this organisation, and when he realized that many of its members were communists he discontinued his association with it. There is no reason to think that Garten has ever held communist views'!

Finally, on 26 June 1947 his Naturalization Certificate was granted and Hugo became a British subject and swore an Oath of Allegiance to the Crown. Hugo continued to teach at Westminster School for the rest of his professional career. He was very musical and put on a number of school plays and operas. He continued to write academic books, particularly on Wagner and Modern German Drama.

Many pages back I mentioned my initial contact with the Institute for German and Romantic Studies ('IGRS'), the Department of London University to which my aunt Anne had given my uncle Hugo's papers. They were kind enough to show a genuine interest not only in his papers but also in such information as I was able to provide about his background, and they invited me to visit them. I learnt from them that when Hugo first came to England in March 1938 he got back together with an old émigré colleague from Vienna called Rudolf Müller. Rudolf was better known by his stage name Martin Miller, and between them and a few others they established an émigré theatre in Hampstead called the *Laterndl*, based on the underground theatre they had previously founded in Vienna. The theatre put on sketches in German and English which would appeal to much the same émigré audience as they had previously had in Vienna. Amongst the Laterndl papers at the IGRS were several of Hugo's handwritten scripts for those sketches. It so happened that shortly after my visit the IGRS put on an exhibition of Martin Miller's works to which I was invited, and many of Hugo's manuscripts were included in the items on display.

Chapter Four: Between the Wars

Amongst the many items unearthed in the metal trunk found in my mother's attic were three documents in particular which looked of interest. But they were all in German and all in manuscript. The German did not present as big a problem as the handwriting, but the combination of the two made it quite impossible for me to translate them. If I was to continue my research, I realised I needed a fully bilingual translator.

As luck would have it, the IGRS (where Hugo's papers were stored) knew just such a person, someone who did translation work for them called Antonia Brotchie, and they arranged a meeting. I gave all three documents to her and she said she would be delighted to translate them. In fact the more she read them, the more interested she said she became, and initially she refused to accept any payment for her work. She even said that when she needed a break from her other work, she would turn to the items I had given her as a form of relaxation! (By the time she got to the third document she conceded that it was a larger job than she had anticipated, and she let me persuade her to accept proper remuneration!)

The document she chose to start with was a diary kept by my grandmother Lisi during the first nine months of the war, at the start of which she was living in Bardwell Road, Oxford. The diary starts on 1 September 1939, two days before war was declared, with the following words:

'Oxford. I feel so relieved, almost happy to be here. Despite all the tension, despite the threat of war! ..... How good it is to be here. In a pretty, well-kept Oxford home, with gentle disciplined people, I am happy with my friendly room, where I can have all my things.'

But it is the diary of a woman who has suffered, overlaid with sadness and regret for a life that never was.

By the time I came to know Lisi she was living near us in London, in a service flat in Harrington Gardens, South Kensington. I remember her as a small elderly lady, always dressed in black, often in a heavy fur coat and with a hat kept in place by a large silver hatpin. Her eyesight was very poor and she wore particularly thick glasses. The rooms of her flat were rather dark and gloomy, with heavy tasselled tablecloths and covers on the furniture. These images are so very different from the rather more glamorous picture of her (now discovered) earlier life, that it was hard for me to imagine her as a person with a romantic past. I cannot remember any real conversations with her.

Lisi Konigsgarten

Lisi died in 1956 when I was nine, and although I remember her as a kindly soul who showed a genuine interest in Tessa and me, my youth and her age were such that I never really got to know her or learnt anything significant about her, still less about her past. With hindsight now I wonder whether she ever really came to terms with the horrors she must have witnessed, the family losses that she suffered, and the new life that she had been forced to flee to in England. The discovery of a diary of hers, therefore, and the details provided by her naturalization file, together provided a more complete picture of her than anything that I had been able to gather either from my own acquaintance with her or from information passed on by my parents. It was like a jigsaw coming together. (The translated diary is reproduced in Appendix II of this book.)

* * *

There was also one more source of information that I was beginning at this time to discover - address records for Berlin and Vienna. Much to my amazement, detailed records are available for all the relevant years, either directly online via scanned directories or by enquiry of the local archive offices. From these records I was able to establish Lisi's movements pretty accurately.

She was born in Brno on 7 August 1881. Her parents were Heinrich and Eugenie Brück. On 5 April 1903 she married Fritz Königsgarten, and they moved into the family home at 55 Dornych next to the factory, where Fritz was being trained to take over the family business. In his 'chronicle' Ignatz writes the following (one must ignore the glowing terms – they are applied to every family member!):

[Fritz] did his apprenticeship with the Erste Brünner Maschinenfabriks Gesellschaft (First Brünn Machine Factory Company) and started work in his father's sheet-metal factory aged 20

(i.e.. in 1889). *Aged not quite 21, he became a partner/shareholder in this firm 'Ig. Königsgarten', a role in which he proved himself brilliantly. He furthered the expansion of the firm with the production of lead pipes and other lead products. He also took an active and successful interest in the more minor activities of the firm.'*

Fritz Konigsgarten

On 13 April 1904 Lisi and Fritz had their first child, Hugo. Then three years later, on 16 May 1907, Lisi had her second child, my father Henry. Hugo states in his naturalization application that he was born in 55 Dornych, the family home, so it seems very likely that my father was born there too. I believe also that Lisi may have had an English governess for the children, as my father once said that due to her he spoke English almost before he spoke German. We know that Henry's father was not Fritz, but Ernst. How did this come about? Fritz died, after a serious illness (we do not know what), on 18 January 1908. The newspaper announcement of his death states it was a short illness, so sometime towards the end of 1907 he must have become ill. It is possible that his younger brother Ernst may have come to live with the family during that time to help look after him, but his critical liaison with Lisi must have been during the summer of 1906, a long time earlier.

Lisi at the wheel of the family car (around 1908?) – apparently the first car in Brno

Maybe it was a brief romance following Ernst's Olympic success in April 1906, or maybe it had been going on for longer. One will never know. But one way or another there was a liaison, and my father was the result. Needless to say, Ignatz's 'chronicle' (written in 1916) makes no mention of this liaison! Henry is clearly referred to as Fritz's second son, again in most glowing terms:

'Heinz Emil Königsgarten, the second son, leads us equally to expect the most noble of characters.'

At what stage, or age, my father was told that Ernst was his true father I do not know, but my father always said that

Ernst treated him like a son or at least took a special interest in him. Ernst was a bachelor, and never married.

Ernst (L) and Lisi (R) skiing together November 1909

In 1911, for reasons I do not know, Lisi and her two boys moved to Vienna. She lived in the 9th District, first in the Garnisongasse and then in the Frankgasse. Then in August 1914 (just before the outbreak of war) while on holiday at Lake Karersee, in what was then the Austrian Dolomites but is now part of Italy, Lisi met Max Bohne, a merchant banker from Berlin. On 1 April 1915 they got married; according to her naturalization application, in Berlin. However, according to the Vienna Stadtarchiv Lisi and her two sons left Vienna on 5 April, but that was probably just when she ceased to be registered there. It makes one wonder, however, if the two small boys attended their mother's second wedding or not. Again one will never know. In Berlin they all moved in with Max.

Discovering the date of her marriage to Max came as really quite a surprise to me, for it meant that my father had spent much more of his childhood in Berlin than I had ever realised. I had had a vague idea that my father had at some stage been to school in Berlin, but not from the age of eight. My father had always talked about Vienna as though it was where he had grown up and the city of his youth, but it now turned out that he had really only lived there for four years, between the ages of four and eight, hardly the most formative years of his life. Yes, he may have returned there in the holidays to visit Ernst, but Berlin, where he lived for his formative school years, must have had at least as much of an influence on him as Vienna. Yet he never spoke of Berlin. He mentioned that he went to University in Leipzig, but it was as though in later life he blocked out completely his upbringing in Germany and remembered only his connection with Austria.

Ernst remained, needless to say, in Vienna, but spent the summers in Altaussee.

As for Max, his name appears in the Berlin address books from before his marriage to Lisi in 1915 until 1934. For most of that time Max and Lisi lived in 46 Brandenburgische Strasse in the district of Wilmersdorf, now part of Charlottenburg. This was, and is, an affluent and leafy residential district on the west side of Berlin, and home to a large percentage of Jewish families, then and now. It adjoins the large central park known as the Tiergarten (not because it is a zoo, although there is a zoo on its northern side, but because it was an ancient hunting ground for the Electors of Brandenburg under the Holy Roman Empire).

The two boys went to school in Berlin, and initially to university there too. Hugo went on to Heidelberg where he obtained a Doctorate in Philosophy in 1930. He then worked as a freelance writer in Berlin until 1933 when he moved back to Vienna and established a career as a writer and theatre critic. My father, Henry, went on to Leipzig University and obtained a Doctorate in Law in 1929, at the young age of 22, before coming to London at the end of that year.

All may have started off comfortably when Lisi and her two boys first moved to Berlin, but they were destined to live through one of the most horrific periods of history. Politically and economically Germany went through a tumultuous time between the wars. In the 1920s inflation affected almost every country in the world, but none so badly as Germany. I would like to take up a few pages here to describe it.

Henry in France in 1930s and in Altaussee in 1949

To do so I can do no better than rely heavily on a series of short extracts from Sebastian Haffner's personal account in his book *Defying Hitler*. It is extraordinary for me to think that my father (who was exactly the same age as Sebastian Haffner) actually lived through all this too and must have seen it with the same eyes.

'1923 was an extraordinary year in Germany. All nations went through the Great War, and most of them have also experienced revolutions, social crises, strikes, redistribution of wealth and

currency devaluation. None but Germany has undergone the fantastic, grotesque extreme of all these together, the gigantic carnival dance of death, the unending bloody Saturnalia, in which not only money but all standards lost their value. The year 1923 prepared Germany, not specifically for Nazism, but for any fantastic adventure.........

The fluctuation of the dollar was the barometer by which, with a mixture of anxiety and excitement, we measured the fall of the mark......... By the end of 1922, prices had gradually risen to between ten and a hundred times the pre-war peacetime level, and the dollar stood at about 500 marks. This, however, had happened gradually. Wages, salaries and prices in general had risen at the same pace........ But the mark now went on the rampage. The dollar shot to 20,000 marks, rested there for a time, jumped to 40,000, paused again and then, with small periodic fluctuations, coursed through the ten thousands and then the hundred thousands.......

Suddenly we discovered that this phenomenon had devastated the fabric of our daily lives. Anyone who had savings in a bank, bonds or gilts, saw their value disappear overnight........ Traders followed hard on the heels of the dollar. A pound of potatoes which yesterday had cost 50,000 marks now cost 100,000. The salary of 65,000 marks brought home the previous Friday was no longer sufficient to buy a packet of cigarettes on Tuesday......

The old and unworldly had the worst of it. Many were driven to begging, many to suicide. The young and quick-witted did well. Overnight they became free, rich and independent...... Amid all the misery, despair and poverty there was an air of light-headed youthfulness, licentiousness and a carnival atmosphere. Now, for once, the young had money and the old did not. Moreover, its nature had changed. Its value lasted only a few hours. It was spent as never before...... But there was another side to the picture. There were beggars everywhere and robbery and burglary occurred on a grand scale.'

Sebastian Haffner describes how each month on the day his father received his salary, his father would write as many cheques as he could for rent, school fees etc, and then the next morning the entire family, including the maid, would get up at 4 or 5 a.m. and go to the wholesale market by taxi. There, in a giant shopping spree, all the rest of his father's salary would be spent on non-perishable foodstuffs in an hour, piled into the taxi, and they would return home in time for school, provisioned for a month's siege.

Everyone searched for a saviour, and there were many who claimed to be one. This was the time of Hitler's Munich putsch. It may have failed, but it was a sign of things to come. A new German mark was introduced and inflation was eventually brought under control, but the whole experience had changed the nature of the German people. Old values no longer applied and people came to accept things which before would not have been tolerated. To quote Robert Gellately in his book *Backing Hitler*:

'The German people, despising Weimar politicians who had utterly failed to reach out to them, found themselves ready to place their trust and understanding in someone who could re-connect them to what they felt were the sounder elements of German traditions.'

* * *

After a period of continual political turbulence, Hitler came to power on 5 March 1933. Prior to the end of February he could not count on obtaining an overall majority in the Reichstag (the German Parliament) on account of the strength of the Communists. But then there was the Reichstag fire, the true circumstances of which have been shrouded in mystery ever since. On the evening of 27 February the Reichstag building was set on fire in an act of arson. That much is certain. Hitler immediately blamed the Communists and ordered the SA to round up as many Communists as they could – in the event nearly 4,000 – and ordered the leaders to be shot, claiming that he was saving the nation from chaos and catastrophe. The next day he went to see President Hindenburg and convinced him that the fire was part of a Communist plot to overthrow the State. Hindenburg agreed to pass what became known as the Reichstag Fire Decree. This banned all Communist publications and outlawed the Communist party, denying them the right to take part in the forthcoming election.

Without Communist opposition on 5 March the Nazis gained 44%. The German National Peoples' Party, which supported the Nazis, gained 8%, thus giving Hitler an overall majority. He was then able to pass what was called the Enabling Act on 23 March 1933 giving himself the power to pass laws independently of the Reichstag for a period of four years, thus effectively creating himself Dictator.

Hitler did not delay long before stamping his mark on the country. His first move was to impose a boycott of Jews and Jewish businesses as from 1 April. To quote again from Sebastian Haffner:

'It had been thought up by Hitler and Goebbels over tea and biscuits at the Obersalzberg in Bavaria the Sunday before. On Monday the papers carried the peculiarly ironic headlines 'Mass Demonstrations Announced'. From Saturday 1 April, they said, all Jewish shops would be boycotted. SA troops would stand guard in front of them and prevent anyone from going in. All Jewish doctors and lawyers were also to be boycotted. SA patrols would check their consulting rooms to ensure that the ruling was obeyed.'

Further measures were added in the next few days. The so-called 'justification' for these measures was as a defence to the 'horror stories' that German Jews were alleged to have spread abroad. But the people no longer needed, or paid any attention to, excuses or justification. Pamphlets, posters and meetings spread poisonous Nazi propaganda and people became numbed to actions which would previously have caused them to stir.

Perhaps the next dramatic event was the burning of the books. On 10 May 1933, following a month-long nationwide campaign, crowds of students and SA stormtroopers started bonfires in over 30 university towns and burnt thousands of books declared to be 'unGerman'. Over 25,000 volumes are thought to have been destroyed. In Berlin a crowd of 40,000 people, singing and chanting Nazi anthems, watched as troops, police and students threw books onto a huge bonfire, while Goebbels declared:

*'The era of extreme Jewish intellectualism is now at an end.......
From this wreckage the phoenix of a new spirit will triumphantly rise.'*

The works consigned to the flames included books by over 75 German and foreign authors. One such author was the German-Jewish poet Heinrich Heine, who in 1821 had prophetically written in one of his plays: 'Where they burn books, they will in the end also burn people'. (I first saw this quote when visiting the concentration camp at Dachau while I was a student in Munich in 1966, where it is poignantly inscribed at the entrance to the camp's main building.)

And thus the repression began. Nazi officials were put in controlling positions of all ministries, local agencies, boards of large companies, committees etc. Judges, who could now be ousted at a moment's notice, were told that their powers had been immeasurably increased. They had become 'people's judges'. They need no longer anxiously follow the letter of the law. Indeed it was better if they did not.

Against this background many resorted to flight and to emigration. My father Henry had already left in 1929 (for England). I am not certain exactly when in 1933 Hugo left Germany (for Vienna), but Lisi left sometime prior to 16 April 1933, on which date she first appears back in Vienna. Max did not finally leave until January 1934. To obtain a further feel for the life they left behind in Berlin at that time, one can do no better than to quote Haffner again. He writes, even as an Aryan, in 1939:

'The plight of non-Nazi Germans in the summer of 1933 was certainly one of the most difficult a person can find himself in: a

condition in which one is hopelessly, utterly overwhelmed, accompanied by the shock of having been caught completely off balance. We were in the Nazis' hands for good or ill. All lines of defence had fallen, any collective resistance had become impossible. Individual resistance was only a form of suicide......

I had lost my friends, had seen harmless acquaintances changed into virtual murderers or enemies, threatening to deliver me to the Gestapo. I had seen all my small daily pleasures vanish. Solidly based institutions like the Prussian justice system had caved in before my eyes. The world of books and discussion groups had dissolved...... Intellectual achievements, the fruits of decades of experience - with a stroke of the pen they had been declared null and void..... Not only that, but the foundations on which such things could be built or replaced had been washed away.'

In grotesque Orwellian fashion, laws with 'doublespeak' names were introduced. A decree called the 'Law for the Re-establishment of the Civil Service' allowed civil servants to be demoted, laid off or sacked without a pension. Those who remained had to complete a detailed questionnaire, stating (amongst other things) what political parties, organisations and associations they had ever belonged to in their lives. The questionnaire finished with a declaration required to be signed, confirming that they 'stood behind the government of national uprising without reservation'. Failure to answer any part of the questionnaire in full would lead to the loss of their job and any pension.

Lisi and Max must have felt lucky to get out when they did. What their financial situation was I do not know. How they fared through the years of inflation I shall never know, but clearly Berlin was not a place for Jews after 1933. It seems that Max only rented their apartment in the Brandenburgische Strasse and so perhaps it would not have been too difficult a move to make. Vienna would have seemed a much better bet, and of course Ernst was there. Judging by the neighbourhood in which they settled, and the fact that they appear to have lived separately from time to time, they must have still been reasonably well off, but whether Max was able to carry on any sort of professional life in Vienna I do not know. Somehow I doubt it.

Although it appears that by this time their marriage was no longer what it had been, they continued to live, if not together, then near each other. Lisi arrived in Vienna on 16 April 1933. The records show her as coming from Brno, but how long she had been there is not stated. It could have been just a few days or it could have been longer. She would presumably have been visiting her mother. She found a flat in the Technikergasse in the 4th District. Max seems to have joined her for a week in the Parkhotel Hübner on 13 June, a grand hotel near the Schönbrunn palace, before returning back to Berlin. On 1 July Lisi leaves Vienna, probably for the summer, and stays in Attnang Puchheim, the home of her brother and sister-in-law Ernst and Irma Brück, for at least some of the time (perhaps the

whole summer), until she returns again to Vienna on 21 October, again to the 4th District, where she is eventually joined by Max in January 1934. By February 1934 they had found an apartment together in the Wohllebengasse, an affluent street near the Schwarzenbergplatz and the Belvedere Palace, on the edge of Vienna's 1st district. It was also just round the corner from Ernst's flat in Argentinierstrasse and Hugo's flat in Prinz Eugen Strasse.

Over the next four years they moved flats a number of times, and sometimes, from the address records, it seems they may even have had separate flats, but they were always near each other and always in the same immediate vicinity. Although their relationship may not have been what it once was, my cousin Thea remembers Max and Lisi visiting Altaussee together when she was there, so they and Ernst must have all been on good terms. But as to whether Max and Lisi stayed with Ernst in the Villa Königsgarten while in Altaussee (which conjures up an interesting scenario!), or separately in a hotel, Thea cannot recall.

Even in Austria the years between 1933 and 1938 would have been a worrying time for them all. Not only would events in Germany have caused them all huge concern, especially Max whose home it was, but in Austria too a huge air of uncertainty hung over its future. Unification with Germany had been forbidden by the Treaty of Versailles, but there was large support for annexation. Austrian Nazis carried out a number of terrorist attacks within the country between 1934 and 1938, and following an ultimatum by Hitler on 11 March 1938, Chancellor Schuschnigg resigned and in effect allowed the Nazis to stage a coup d'état. On 12 March German tanks rolled into Austria and on 15 March 1938 Hitler himself arrived in Vienna, having crossed the border at his birthplace in Braunau, and gave a triumphal speech welcoming Austria into the German Reich. Although subsequently it suited all parties to claim that Austria was the first victim of Nazi aggression, the fact is that this annexation (*Anschluss*) was hugely popular. Hitler's troops were welcomed by ecstatic crowds cheering and throwing flowers.

But for Ernst, Max, Lisi and Hugo the Anschluss did not bode well. Hugo was in the most danger. Not only did the Nazis immediately introduce anti-Jewish laws and restrictions, but Hugo and his underground theatre group had been writing anti-Hitler sketches and producing plays poking fun at the Nazis and their rhetoric. He realised he was a prime candidate for arrest, imprisonment or deportation. He tried to telephone a number of friends from his theatre group, but there was no answer from any of them. He decided they had either been arrested or fled. He took no chances and left the next day, 13 March. His wife Anne told me that Hugo's train was one of the last to be allowed into Switzerland, but not everybody got across the border. When the train stopped at the last station before the frontier all those with Austrian passports were removed from the train, and it was only thanks to his Czech passport that Hugo managed to remain on board. Once over the border, bottles of champagne were broken open and there was huge rejoicing, but of course tinged with a great sense of unease over the fate of those who had been forcibly removed. Anne went on to say that two days later the Gestapo came to arrest Hugo. He had fled just in time. I was subsequently able to confirm the timing of his departure, first by one of Lisi's stories that Antonia had translated, and secondly by a letter of Hugo's that I found in the Vienna archives in May 2014 in which he gave the date he left Vienna as indeed 13 March 1938. Thanks to my father already living in England and able to act as a financial guarantor, Hugo was then able to get an entry visa into England.

From the Vienna City archives I was also able to establish that Lisi continued to live in the Wohllebengasse until 30 August 1938, while from the National Archives in Kew I had established that she had arrived in England on 8 September. By what route she travelled I do not know. In her diary written almost exactly a year later (see Appendix II) she refers on the opening page to the horrors of Berlin that she left behind, so whether that intervening week was spent in Berlin, or whether she was referring to the Berlin of 1933, or whether in fact she really meant Vienna, I shall probably never know.

I was also able to discover from the Vienna archives that Lisi had succeeded in obtaining an export licence for 23 items. These included one oil painting, 11 water colours, various other drawings and paintings, one antique clock and a 'glass box'. The permit was granted on 9 August 1938. It is stamped by the Wien Ostbahnhof (Vienna's East Station) on 30 August and by Customs Control on the German border at Passau on 2

September. The permit rather unusually doesn't give the address to which the items are to be exported, it merely gives her name as the recipient, but Passau is on a straight-line route to the Channel ports, and not to Berlin or Czechoslovakia. These items would have eventually been with her in her flat in Harrington Gardens, South Kensington, after the war, which I remember well as a child having a distinctive Austrian feel about it.

But in any event, she had left Max behind. As touched on earlier, this raises a number of questions. Had their relationship broken down irretrievably? Had he tried to get an exit visa and failed? But she, after all, had another reason for coming. She had two sons in London. He did not. Or, given that he did not have the same family ties, did he simply think that he would survive alright in Vienna? After all Thea and Robert were still there at that time and so was Ernst. It wasn't until October or November that the last of them felt the need to leave.

But Max's life in Vienna was about to take a dramatic turn for the worse. Whether he had been able to work at all since his arrival in Vienna in 1933 I do not know, but things were about to become much more difficult. While those who had somewhere to flee to and could do so, did so, Max probably found himself with nowhere to go. I discovered from Lisi's diary that Max had been hoping to flee to Budapest in October 1939, but for reasons unknown he never succeeded. From the comfort of the Wohllebengasse (literally 'Good Living Street') he was forced to move into ever smaller and more uncomfortable surroundings. Via a series of boarding houses and hostels he ended up in a one-room flat in No.8 Negerlegasse, which still stands (as a building at least) to this day. It was from the Negerlegasse that he was finally deported on 20 August 1942 to Theresienstadt. He died there at four in the morning on 23 July 1943. His death certificate – yes, despite the thousands of deaths that occurred, the Camp authorities still managed to complete detailed death certificates – states the cause of death as tuberculosis.

There is an extraordinary little anecdote relating to my research into the fate of Max. When I was trawling the Internet for information I came across a reference to the fact that some flowers had been left a few years back on the steps of No.8 Negerlegasse by a certain Dr. Wolfgang Perr from Bad Ischl. There was no explanation why, or what his connection with Max was, so I googled Dr. Perr and found a phone number for him and phoned him. He was a teacher, and he explained that he personally had no connection with Max, but that he had taken a group of schoolchildren on an outing related to the Holocaust, and that they had put flowers outside a number of addresses which they had randomly selected from a list of victims whose last known addresses they had been able to establish. Max's just happened to be one of them and that's why they had placed their flowers there. I explained my connection and thanked him warmly.

It is clear from Lisi's diary that she did not know the fate of Ernst or Max (or many others) until after the war, when information was made available by the Red Cross. Despite the fact that she and Max may well have been 'separated' (to use a modern term) by the time she left Vienna, she still agonised in her diary over what might have become of him. It is also clear that there had been another man in her life after him (by the name of Pfeiffer) but I have not been able to establish anything more about him. The fact is that she had lost her first husband, Fritz, on his death in 1908, she had had to leave her one-time lover Ernst and her second husband Max to their fates in Vienna in 1938, and she had also left at some stage another man Pfeiffer with whom she had been at some time amorously involved. Finally she had left her mother Eugenie still living in Brno, and very soon any further communication with her would have been impossible. Her mother too would ultimately perish in Theresienstadt on 15 April 1942. Lisi must have come to England a sad, if not traumatised, woman and her diary of 1939/40 clearly reflects this.

* * *

The second document to be translated by Antonia was assumed to be a novel. Indeed when I first handed the documents to Antonia, I had assumed the first two to have both been written by Hugo (the diary and the novel), as the third was a letter to Hugo and also I knew Hugo had lived in Oxford during the war and the diary was clearly written there. So it had been a surprise when Antonia pointed out that the diary was clearly that of a woman. The handwriting was the same in both documents, so the novel must have been written by her too. It was entitled *Last Days in Vienna* and began with the arrival of Nazi troops, so I then assumed it was a story based on fact about her last months in Vienna. But when Antonia translated it, it became clear that it did not relate to her last days, but those of a young man in love with a girl whom he had had to leave behind on his hurried departure. In the story this young man had fled Vienna by train on the day after the Anschluss. It was therefore clearly a story about Hugo, but was it fact or fiction? In the story she describes the view out of the window of the young man's flat and how it overlooked the Belvedere Palace. I had assumed that as she lived near the Belvedere (but not overlooking it) she had chosen this description because it sounded romantic. But when I visited Vienna in May 2014 and discovered a letter from Hugo in the Archives in which he gave his last address in Vienna as No.16 Prinz Eugen Strasse (now the Monaco Embassy) and visited that address, I could see that any flat above ground floor level did indeed directly overlook the Belvedere and its gardens.

Here then was the story of Hugo's dramatic flight from Vienna, with all the elements of a romantic thriller. It ends with the character in the story thinking he was about to leave his girlfriend behind, but as he was on the train waiting for it to depart, there she was in the crowd and their eyes meet. She runs towards him and jumps aboard. Whether this final detail was true for Hugo, I shall never know. I did not feel I could ask his widow, my aunt Anne, and anyway she might not have known. Lisi does mention Hugo having a girlfriend in England a year later, in her diary, but whether this was a girl who fled with him from Austria or not, there is no knowing. But the novel does describe dramatically, if somewhat romantically, the terrifying events of those days. (The translated novel is reproduced in Appendix I of this book.)

16 Prinz Eugen Strasse –where Hugo had his flat overlooking the Belvedere Palace

* * *

The third document I had given to Antonia was a 20-page foolscap letter, addressed to Hugo, written in 1948 from Los Angeles. The handwriting was really too difficult to establish anything meaningful about the author or its contents. But once it was translated it appeared to be from a close friend or relation of Hugo's who had also escaped from Austria, in which he described his own dramatic escape, and said how glad he was to have heard from Hugo after so many years, and to have re-established contact. Such was his handwriting that we originally thought his name was Oskar Sellinck, but after a bit of detection work, I discovered that an Oskar Jellinek was the brother of one of Ernst's sisters-in-law (the wife of his elder brother Ludwig). Here was the link and his correct name.

Through Geni I managed to contact a relation of Jellinek's, but she was unable to furnish me with much more information about him or copies of any other correspondence. But there clearly had been further correspondence, if only the initial letter from Hugo re-making contact, which I felt was well worth pursuing as we might find out more about Hugo's own escape. So I re-trawled the internet and put the name 'Jellinek' into Google. Once again I was lucky and up came some results. There was a reference to a book of letters between various authors and writers, which included correspondence to and from Oskar Jellinek, which was held by an academic institution in Germany. The index showed that this book not only included the letter from Oskar to my uncle, but also Hugo's letters to him and other writers.

I wrote to the Institute and managed to obtain copies. I now had not only the complete exchange of correspondence between Hugo and Oskar, but also a list of many other letters of Hugo's to and from German writers and philosophers. But they were all in German and will take time to read. But they were at least typed, so I felt I could do the task myself, over time.

Hugo's letters to Oskar were interesting in a number of respects, as Hugo described his time teaching in Oxford during the war, and the pupils' antipathy to learning about anything German (whereas they took to French quite comfortably), and on the family front he discussed his mother's depression and her worries. He said he found Oxford the only place in England where he felt really at home. In London he missed signs of nature, the trees and the flowers, and compared it unfavourably in that respect with Vienna. He said Vienna was the only place in the world where one could find the happy harmony of town and nature.

Hugo as a young man and later in Oxford

* * *

I also began to research Lisi's family. As a child in London I had known an Uncle Ernst and Aunt Irma, but, as so often with children, one never really knows how relations are connected. After all, there are (or were then) other close family friends, or perhaps one's godparents, whom one called 'Aunt' and 'Uncle', so it was often not clear to me as a child who was a relation and who was not.

But as it turned out Uncle Ernst was a brother of Lisi, and as I discovered from Lisi's naturalization file, they had all shared a house together in Oxford during the war. After the war Lisi came to live in London, and eventually so did Ernst and Irma too.

I was aware as I grew up of Bruck cousins – they dropped the *umlaut* when they came to England – Monica and Peter, who were one family, and Jill, Rosemary and Sheila, who were another. Thanks to Geni, and a family tree drawn up by my mother, I was now able to identify them all. The fathers of the two families were Gerd and Harry, both sons of Ernst and Irma Brück. From my mother's old address book, which I also had, I was able to contact them and re-establish the connection. (In August 2014 John Fisher arranged a meeting for several of us to meet at his flat in London.)

I also built up the family tree on Geni of the other Brück and Mostny cousins. Bruno Mostny (the brother of Aunt Irma) and his wife Mary were my father's generation and about the only close relations who survived the war (they somehow escaped to Brazil for the duration). They lived near Linz where Bruno ran a family business, and always came to visit us in Altaussee when we were there as children. I remembered him particularly as he owned a large American car, which had electric windows and a 'cow horn' (both fascinating toys for a young boy!).

But as well as discovering the connections between the relations that I knew, or had known, I also discovered that there had been other close relations of whom I had known nothing, who had perished in the Holocaust. For example, not only had Lisi lost Ernst, Max and her mother but her sister Marie appears to have died in Theresienstadt too, in 1942. Marie's husband, their daughter, their daughter's husband and 12-year-old son had also all died between 1942 and 1944, after initial deportation to Theresienstadt, either there or in Dachau, Auschwitz or Birkenau. All this information had been posted on Geni by Randy Schoenberg or my cousin John Fisher.

There was one other name I discovered on Geni that was in fact familiar to me. My grandmother Lisi had another sister called Emmy. She did not appear to have died in the Holocaust. She had married a Viennese named Alfred Russo in 1907. I wrote to the Stadtarchiv in Vienna and ascertained that after living in Vienna she and Alfred separated in 1916, and were subsequently divorced, but beyond that there was no further information. Then, by chance, I found that Hugo's letter to Oskar Jellinek of January 1948 that I had obtained from Germany mentioned his aunt Emmy surviving the war and living in Dresden. Suddenly the name Emmy rang a bell. I remembered that there was someone called Emmy whom my parents had kept in touch with during my childhood, and to whom they sent parcels from time to time, who lived in East Germany. I remember once asking why we had never seen her, and being told that East Germany was a country one couldn't get out of, nor could one visit. So there she had to remain, cut off from her family and possibly in some degree of poverty, behind the Iron Curtain. This all now fitted in. She was one of Lisi's sisters. But what eventually became of her I still did not know.

I then read Hugo's letter again and found that I had overlooked the fact that he had mentioned a new surname for her, Mraczek. But who was Mraczek and when had they married? With the assistance of my cousin John Fisher I discovered that she had married the Czech composer Joseph Gustav Mraczek (born in Brno in 1878). Furthermore, after studying in Brno and Vienna, he had moved to Dresden in 1919 where he took up a post at the Conservatory as a teacher of composition and a conductor. So it is likely that she had married him prior to 1919, and that would explain her mysterious move to Dresden. Perhaps she had even known him as a child in Brno? It also meant that she must have lived in Dresden throughout the war, and most probably throughout the firebombing in February 1945. However, with some further research I established that Joseph himself died in Dresden on 24 December 1944, i.e. prior to the bombing. How I do not know. But there was one more surprise. At some later stage Emmy must have managed to escape the Iron Curtain, because John Fisher then found a German newspaper announcement online of her celebrating her 82nd birthday on 23 April 1970 in Reutlingen, West Germany! Since then I have discovered, amongst the family papers, a photograph of Emmy with a message on the back, sent possibly to my parents, from Reutlingen in 1963. So my parents must have known she had escaped the Iron Curtain. I myself drove through Germany with a couple of school friends in 1964, but I do not remember any suggestion that I should look her up. But perhaps I simply wasn't interested at that time in my family's past.

Further investigations have revealed that Emmy died in 1972.

* * *

(During my search through the Holocaust records I in fact came across another Alfred Russo. Also born in Vienna, in 1871, he had been deported from the Fossoli di Corpi camp in Northern Italy to Auschwitz on 22 February 1944, and died there four days later. This had originally been an Italian prisoner-of-war camp, but between December 1943 and March 1944 was turned into a concentration camp for Jews and political opponents of the Italian fascist government. There were two shipments of prisoners from there to Auschwitz. Alfred was on the second shipment along with 650 others. One of those was the Italian writer Primo Levi, who survived the war and describes his experience in his book *If This is a Man* published in 1947. Levi's possible connection with Emmy's husband Russo prompted me to buy the book. It is well worth reading, one of the best of its kind, and for that reason I have left this paragraph in this account, even though this turned out to be a different Alfred Russo.)

Chapter Five: Vienna

It is probably about time that I said a bit more about Ernst. He was after all the rather enigmatic character who sparked off the whole of this research. Despite the fact that we knew he was our father's true father, we knew very little else about him. We knew that he had practised fencing as that was often mentioned; there was a photograph of him (the only photograph we had in fact seen of him) in his fencing clothes; his épée had survived and was in the family attic (it is now in Tessa's house in France); and we knew he had lived in Vienna and that he had a house in Altaussee where he spent the summer and where my father joined him every year; but beyond that we knew almost nothing.

Through Geni I was able to discover that he was born in Brno on 14 July 1880. By further research I was even able to discover the original manuscript registration of his birth. Quite amazingly, all these ancient manuscript volumes have been digitised. Then by a simple Google search I was able to discover his fencing achievements. He had represented Austria in the Summer Olympics in Athens in April 1906, in all three fencing disciplines: épée, sabre, and foil. Aged 25 he was the youngest Austrian participant. I had also found several more photos of him at various stages of his life in the black metal trunk in my mother's attic, and I had found Ignatz's family 'chronicle' which has this glowing description of him:

> 'Following his mercantile studies in Prague, he completed his military year in the Army and obtained the rank of Lieutenant. For his profession he chose that of a leather manufacturer.
>
> He worked first in Lipto, near Miklos (now Miklósi) in Hungary, where he undertook the hardest of physical work, and where he brilliantly acquired complete aptitude and dominated. He then pursued the theoretical expansion of this business with enthusiasm

The one photo we had seen of Ernst in our childhood – in his fencing jacket

and passion in Freiberg, Saxony, and then strove for ultimate perfection in London. From there he intended to go to America. However, in London he was overcome by a persistent eye problem, which upset his plans and above all prevented him from following a profession.

With his unusual and quite special willpower and physical strength he took up at this difficult time the art of fencing. However strange it may sound and incomprehensible it may appear, and despite his defective eyesight, he reached perfection and ranked amongst the best in the art of fencing.

He lives in Vienna and is honoured and respected in the best of circles.'

Unfortunately there are no dates, but more information can be obtained from a sports information website recently available, which states as follows:

'Ernst Königsgarten was an officer in the cavalry reserves in France and was a member of the Riding School of Emperor Franz-Josef (François-Joseph), and a member of la Salle d'Arme of his fencing teacher, Monsieur Della Santa. Königsgarten fenced foil and épée left-handed but fenced sabre, his best weapon, right-handed. He competed in multiple events on the continent, including those at Marienbad in 1905, Praha in 1906, Trieste in 1906, Milano in 1906, Karlsbad in 1907, Ostende in 1907, and Baden-Baden in 1909. He was a member of the Bureau de la Fédération d'Escrime Autrichienne and of the Comité du Wiener Fechtklub.'

He does indeed seem to have achieved considerable heights in the fencing (and riding) world.

In any event, at some stage before 1916 (when Ignatz's chronicle was written) he moved from Brno to Vienna. (He may even have moved at the same time as Lisi, in 1911.) Brno was however only 80 miles from Vienna and this would not therefore have been a major move. Ernst would have doubtless visited Vienna many times in his life (particularly if he was a member of Franz-Joseph's Riding School) and grown up very much aware of its flourishing cultural life. This was rich and exotic. The Emperor Franz Joseph had been on the throne since 1848 and had overseen an enormous growth in the city. He had removed restrictions on Jewish residency and there had been a huge influx of Jewish families from all over the empire. Between 1860 and 1900 the Jewish population of Vienna had exploded from 6,000 to 147,000, the largest in Western Europe. Affluent Jewish families became huge patrons of the arts and filled the theatres, opera houses and art galleries. Vienna had become not only the cultural and artistic centre of Europe (which is why Hitler felt so incensed when he failed the admission test for the Vienna Academy of Fine Arts in 1907), but also the richest city in Europe. But not everyone was rich. Many lived in poverty, and anti-Semitism accompanied the rising influence of the Jewish community. When Hitler left Vienna in 1913 he was imbued with the rhetoric of its anti-Semitic mayor Karl Lueger.

One of Vienna's artists who was making a name for himself at the turn of the century was Gustav Klimt. Although from a Catholic family, he did not share the growing anti-Semitism. In fact the Jewish community provided him with his best patrons. Along with a few others he founded the Secessionist Movement in 1897 and became its first President. It was founded to counter the prevailing conservatism of art at that time, although no one style united its members. Above the Secession Building, opened near the Karlsplatz in 1898, were the words *'Der Zeit Ihre Kunst. Der Kunst Ihre Freiheit'* ('To Every Age Its Art. To Art Its Freedom').

But Klimt was not only a great artist. He was also a great lover and seducer of women. His patrons were the rich Jewish businessmen of Vienna, and many of their wives and daughters fell under his spell. The grander female members of that society provided a rich source of models, and they all sought to have their portraits painted by him. Although Klimt died in 1918 and by then this exotic world would have been fading, this was the Vienna into which Ernst stepped when he moved there. By 1919 he was living in the Schwindgasse and then in 1933 he moved to his flat on the first floor of No.2 Argentinierstrasse.

One of the best-known society hostesses during Ernst's early years in Vienna was Adele Bloch-Bauer, particularly once she had modelled for her two portraits painted by Klimt in 1907 and 1912. The first of these has become known as *The Lady in Gold* and has become an iconic painting of that period and perhaps one of the most recognised paintings in the world. She was almost exactly the same age as Ernst, and given the society in which they both mixed, must have been well known to him. He would have been right in the middle of the social circle inhabited by Klimt's models, and he couldn't fail to have seen the golden portrait of her at one exhibition or another. In 1905

Ernst in white tie, in uniform, and with the Austrian fencing team and their coach in 1909 (on right of group)

Klimt had painted a portrait of Margarete Wittgenstein. The Wittgensteins lived in the Wohllebengasse, the same street as Lisi and just round the corner from Ernst. The Bloch-Bauers lived in No.18 Elisabethstrasse, the other side of the Karlsplatz.

No.2 Argentinierstrasse

The subsequent history of *The Lady in Gold* and the other Klimt paintings collected by Ferdinand and Adele has been much written about recently, and even now made into a film (*Woman in Gold*), but it is perhaps well worth retelling here in brief.

Ferdinand Bloch-Bauer was a Czech sugar magnate, born in Bohemia in 1864, with houses in both Czechoslovakia and Vienna. He was also a prolific art collector. In addition to seven paintings by Klimt, the Bloch-Bauers acquired nine paintings by Waldmüller, three by Schindler and one by Moll. His wife Adele was born in Vienna in 1881 and they married in 1899. Sadly, their only child died one day old in 1904. It is thought that Adele modelled for Klimt not only for her own two portraits, but also for other paintings as well, for example for his 1901 painting *Judith*; the similarity is striking. Over the next few years he made more than a hundred studies of Adele. Few other women received so much of his attention. His first full portrait of her, commissioned by Ferdinand, was the result of several years' work and was completed in 1907. Klimt interwove Adele into an audacious background of gold leaf, almost a modern form of a religious icon. It was an instant success. A Viennese newspaper described the portrait as 'an idol in a golden shrine'. It made Adele, aged 26, an instant celebrity. Adele became a symbol of an enlightened turn-of-the-century Vienna. The Habsburgs often borrowed Adele's portrait for exhibitions, to portray a modern and sophisticated image of their Empire.

Klimt painted a second portrait of Adele, also commissioned by Ferdinand, completed in 1912, but this was a very much more serious image of a more mature woman. If the first portrait was that of a seductive lover, this one showed a woman who demanded respect and signified perhaps the end of their long affair.

Adele died in 1925 (well before the rise of the Nazis) but in her will she requested her husband to leave her five Klimts (her two portraits and three other paintings) to the Austrian State Gallery upon his death. But in 1938, following the Anschluss, Ferdinand fled to Switzerland. He survived the war but died there in 1945, leaving his estate to his nephew Robert and his two nieces Maria and Luise. However, after Ferdinand had fled Austria, the paintings had been seized by the Nazis. Despite the fact that they fell into the category of what the Nazis called 'degenerate art' and should have been destroyed, the shrewd (Austrian) Nazi dealer responsible for their seizure recognised their potential value and gave them to the Belvedere in a secret deal. The gallery's art historians then 're-invented' the two portraits of Adele, removing any reference to her identity. The 1907 portrait was given the title *The Lady in Gold* and after the war was put on permanent display in the Upper Belvedere Palace.

Maria Bloch-Bauer was one of Ferdinand's two nieces, and hence one of his beneficiaries. In 1937 she had married Frederick Altmann and after a dramatic escape from the Nazis they eventually arrived in Los Angeles. (He had also been held hostage for a while in Dachau concentration camp to force his brother to transfer the family textile factory into German hands.) After the war and Ferdinand's death Maria wrote many times to the Austrian government regarding her family's claim to the Klimt paintings but got no reply. At that time she said she would have been happy to leave the paintings on display at the Belvedere if only her family's claim to them had been acknowledged. But it never was. She was faced with a wall of silence. And so the situation remained for over 40 years.

However, eventually, in the 1990s, came the revelation that Austria's president Kurt Waldheim had been a member of the Nazi party, and even of the SS, and Austria came under increasing pressure to be more open about its Nazi past. A new law was introduced by Austria's Green Party requiring greater transparency over the restitution of Nazi-looted artworks. It was as a result of this that the Austrian investigative journalist Hubertus Czernin revealed that Ferdinand Bloch-Bauer had never in fact donated the Klimts to the state museum as the Austrian government had always maintained. The government's case relied solely on the 'request' in Adele's will which they maintained was binding on Ferdinand. Maria maintained that it was not, and that had Adele known of the subsequent seizure and theft of the paintings by the Austrian Government, she would never have made such a request. In any event, by seizing the paintings before Ferdinand's death, the Austrian government had destroyed whatever claim it might have had.

There was in fact one final string to Maria's bow. An invoice had been discovered showing that the paintings were in fact Ferdinand's property and not Adele's, so the wording of her will was in the end irrelevant.

Randol Schoenberg, the grandson of the famous composer, and a budding young lawyer, whose family had also settled in Los Angeles, was a good friend as well as a distant relation of Maria Altmann's, and he brought to Maria's attention in 2000 that a new law in the United States now allowed her to bring proceedings against the Austrian Government in her home country. (Proceedings in Austria had previously been ruled out on account of being prohibitively expensive as they required an upfront fee based on the value of the paintings, which would have amounted to US $1.5 million.) She therefore now authorised him to start proceedings in the United States on a conditional fee basis (i.e. on a percentage of the value of any paintings recovered). The Austrian Government immediately countered by pleading sovereign immunity, but the US courts rejected this argument. After several unsuccessful appeals by the Austrian Government over this question, the US Supreme Court finally ruled in 2004 that Austria was not immune from such a suit. As a result of that decision, Austria and Maria Altmann eventually agreed to have the substantive dispute settled by binding arbitration before three judges in Austria. Eventually in January 2006, amid great excitement on the part of Maria and her supporters, the judges ruled in Altmann's favour and in March of that year the paintings were finally released to Maria and the other family heirs. There was a final, and hugely well-attended, exhibition of the paintings in Vienna, amid much moaning by the media concerning their removal from the country, after which Maria had the paintings shipped to Los Angeles. Such was the value of the shipment that several 'dummy' transports were arranged to throw off any would-be hijackers.

After a brief period of public display in Los Angeles, all the paintings were sent to Christie's for sale in New York. The portrait *Adele Bloch-Bauer I (1907)* was sold privately to Ronald Lauder, heir of the cosmetics business Estée Lauder, for $135 million (the highest price at that time ever paid for a painting) and is now on display in his Neue Galerie in New York. The remaining four paintings were sold at auction to an anonymous buyer for a combined total of $192 million, the painting known as *Adele Bloch-Bauer II (1912)* fetching $87.9 million.

The conditional fee agreement between Maria Altmann and Randol Schoenberg entitled Schoenberg to 40% of the value of the works recovered. This was an enormous sum, but he had given up six years of his life and lost his partnership position with his law firm as a result. The rest was split equally between Maria and the other heirs or their children. Thea's husband Robert Bloch-Bauer had long since died (and they had in fact previously divorced) but their son George received his due share of the proceeds. Maria died in February 2011, just a few days short of her 95th birthday.

The dramatic journey of the Lady in Gold, from Klimt's studio in Vienna to Christie's in New York, could not possibly have been imagined by Ernst when he moved to Vienna sometime prior to 1916. And my father, who died in 1988, would not have known of the eventual recovery of the painting either. But what is surprising is that my father never mentioned the painting to us as children, even though I clearly remember visiting the Belvedere with him in 1960, where the painting would have been hanging. (It has to be said however that Klimt would not have been amongst my father's favourite artists!)

I have also asked Thea what she knew of the painting in her youth. It will be remembered that although she was not born until 1918, she had married Adele's nephew Robert in 1937. Yet she now thinks she was not aware of the painting until Maria started her action for its recovery. The Belvedere must have done a very good job indeed at re-inventing the painting and obliterating any reference to its past. Maria alone was the only family survivor to have remembered its true origin.

* * *

I know very little about Ernst's life from the time he moved to Vienna until 1938. From 1914 to 1918 Austria was at war (in particular fighting on the southern front against Italy) and life would have been tough even for those at home, with shortages and hardships. Defeat in 1918 and the collapse of the Austro-Hungarian Empire would have been a bitter blow. The empire was broken up under the Treaty of Versailles and the constituent countries were given their independence. The German-speaking population of the new Czechoslovakia were not made to feel very welcome and that may well be why my father and Hugo adopted Czech nationality so as to make visits to Brno and their grandfather easier. Little did they know what a benefit, not to say a lifeline, this would turn out to be twenty years later. But, unlike many others, Ernst must have had some money to spare following the end of the First World War, because in 1919 he bought the house in Altaussee. It had previously belonged to the von Binzer family, who had owned the neighbouring house as well, but who, as a result of the war, were not in a financial position to retain it. Ernst would have been 39 at the time he bought it.

As in Germany, life in Vienna between the wars was not easy, and the economy there too suffered from hyper-inflation. Nevertheless, as I understand it, Ernst spent every summer in Altaussee and my father joined him there for all or part of it. The rest of the year Ernst spent in Vienna, and perhaps my father joined him there too occasionally – sadly I never thought to ask.

It was during this inter-war period that Thea also visited Altaussee with her family, and the photograph was taken of her father, my father, her mother and her, all in swimming costumes by the lake. And it was during this same period that she remembers Max and Lisi visiting too.

In the 1930s Austria was divided between those who wanted the country integrated into a 'Greater Germany' and those who wanted it to remain independent. There were marches and counter-marches, demonstrations and counter-demonstrations. In July 1934 Chancellor Dollfuss, who supported an independent Austria, was assassinated in an attempted Nazi '*Putsch*', and his successor Schuschnigg was not strong enough to resist Hitler's demands. In July 1936 he was forced into signing a very ambiguous treaty with Germany and over the next twenty months the Nazi influence became greater and greater. By 1938 Austrian Nazis were throwing petrol and smoke bombs into synagogues and daubing swastikas and Nazi slogans on the walls of houses. Mobs roamed the streets molesting anyone they took to be Jewish. Following a heated meeting with Hitler at Berchtesgaden in February, Schuschnigg was forced into appointing Nazi supporters into his cabinet. When Schuschnigg announced a plebiscite on the issue of Austrian independence in March, Hitler issued an ultimatum that the plebiscite be called off and a new Chancellor appointed to be approved by the German Government. Wishing to avoid bloodshed, Schuschnigg capitulated and ordered the army not to resist, and on 12 March 1938 German troops marched into Austria.

We know that Hugo fled Vienna on 13 March. We know that Lisi left for England on 30 August. We think that my father went out to Vienna in the autumn of that year to urge other family members to leave too. We know that Thea and her family left on 20 October. Ernst obviously soon felt it was time for him to leave too.

Prior to that time Germany had threatened only that part of Czechoslovakia known as the Sudetenland. This was a relatively narrow strip of territory adjoining the German border of Czechoslovakia and inhabited by German-speaking people. These people had never been happy at finding themselves as a minority group in the new Czechoslovakia after 1919, and their 'protection' had been Hitler's excuse for demanding the annexation of the Sudetenland. These demands gave rise to the Munich Conference in September 1938, attended by Hitler, Mussolini, Chamberlain and the French Prime Minister

Daladier, at which England and France had reluctantly agreed, in order to preserve peace, to allow Hitler to occupy the Sudetenland in return for a promise by him not to invade the rest of Czechoslovakia. This conference had resulted in the famous 'piece of paper' brandished by Chamberlain on his arrival back in England, which he boldly declared 'confirmed the determination of our two peoples never to go to war with one another again'. German occupation of the Sudetenland followed immediately in October. Unfortunately Chamberlain's bold confidence, or many would subsequently say his naïvety, would haunt him for the rest of his life and ultimately lead to his resignation.

Churchill's speech to the House of Commons at that time, denouncing the Agreement, is well worth recording:

'We have suffered a total and unmitigated defeat ... you will find that in a period of time which may be measured by years, but may be measured by months, Czechoslovakia will be engulfed in the Nazi régime. We are in the presence of a disaster of the first magnitude ... we have sustained a defeat without a war, the consequences of which will travel far with us along our road ... we have passed an awful milestone in our history, when the whole equilibrium of Europe has been deranged, and that the terrible words have for the time being been pronounced against the Western democracies: 'Thou art weighed in the balance and found wanting'. And do not suppose that this is the end. This is only the beginning of the reckoning. This is only the first sip, the first foretaste of a bitter cup which will be proffered to us year by year unless by a supreme recovery of moral health and martial vigour, we arise again and take our stand for freedom as in the olden time.'

And on 3 October 1938:

'England has been offered a choice between war and shame. She has chosen shame, and will get war.'

What prophetic words.

On 9 November a series of coordinated attacks against Jews and Jewish property took place throughout Germany and Austria. Many synagogues and Jewish shops were smashed and burnt in an operation which became known as 'Kristallnacht'. The authorities looked on without intervening and the fire brigades were instructed not to put out the fires, but merely to prevent them from spreading to neighbouring non-Jewish buildings.

Nevertheless, in the light of the Munich Agreement, Czechoslovakia must have seemed a safer place than Vienna, and so on 20 November 1938 Ernst left No.2 Argentinierstrasse for the last time and moved back to Brno. What is quite surprising however is that he also managed to have some of his belongings sent there too. One of the documents that I was able to uncover in the Vienna archives was an export permit obtained by Ernst dated 5 October 1938 for two oil paintings and six engravings or prints. Whether there were other items as well which did not require an export permit or whether these were the only items taken or allowed to be taken to Brno I do not know, but permission was obtained from the necessary authorities, complete with Nazi seals, for these items to be exported to the Königsgarten family home in Brno. One page of the permit bears a stamp from Wien Ostbahnhof (Vienna's East Railway Station) dated 26 November 1938 and a stamp of the Railway Customs Control at the Czechoslovakian border dated 1 December. Ernst would by then have been in Brno to receive the items.

The assumption from the above permit, and what seems most probable in any event, is that Ernst moved into the family home at 55 Dornichgasse (to give it its German name) which at that time was the home of his brother Ludwig, who had some years earlier taken over the family firm and the house with it.

But such stability was not to last. The rest of Czechoslovakia was invaded by Hitler in March 1939, effectively trapping Ernst within it, and sealing his fate. After that, life would have got more and more uncomfortable. In July 1941 Ludwig was required to sell the family business (and quite possibly the house too) to the Aryan owners of a rival metal company based in a small town 50 km northeast of Brno. My visit to the archive offices in Brno produced a photocopy of the sale and purchase agreement. It contains the following clause:

'The seller is Jewish. The contract is therefore subject to official approval and is only valid if all necessary permits are granted.'

That wording of course conceals a lot more than it gives away. The reason for the sale is not hard to imagine.

Whether Ernst and Ludwig also had to move out of the family house is not clear, but either way it was not long before Ernst was on the move again, and on this occasion for the last time. On 5 December 1941, at the age of 61, he was deported to Theresienstadt, some 170 miles to the north. The deportations to Theresienstadt (now called Terezin) had only just started. The first had been on 24 November from Prague. Ernst's transport No. K-605 was the fifth such transport overall, and the second from Brno. Each transport consisted of between 1,000 and 1,200 prisoners. Of Ernst's transport of 1,000 prisoners only 68 survived.

Chapter Six: Theresienstadt

Much information is available on the Internet and in books about life and conditions in Theresienstadt, so I will not describe the appalling and miserable conditions in any detail, but a few paragraphs may be helpful. I visited the town in May 2014 and saw it clearly for myself.

The town of Theresienstadt consists of two fortresses, both built in the late 18th century as defensive strongholds following several Prussian-Austrian wars. The Small Fortress was used as a prison during World War I, housing amongst others Gavrilo Prinzip, the assassin of Franz Ferdinand in 1914, while the Main Fortress was used as a garrison town. In June 1940 the Small Fortress became a police prison for the Prague Gestapo. Over 30,000 political prisoners and members of various resistance groups passed through its gates, suffering famine, epidemics, torture and execution. Over 2,600 died or were executed, while a further 5,500 died after deportation to other concentration camps.

The Main Fortress was turned into a ghetto, collection and transit camp. Over 155,000 prisoners were detained in the camp between November 1941 and May 1945, of whom 35,000 died there and a further 83,000 after deportation elsewhere. Thousands more continued to die even in the weeks after the war ended from epidemics and diseases, such as typhus and spotted fever.

As the first transports began to arrive in November 1941, the previous inhabitants were moved out, and all civilians had to be out by mid-1942. Whereas imprisoned Jews had been held in barrack buildings before this date, the entire town now became a large prison. But there were certain areas such as the centre of the main square where Jews were not allowed to tread.

A barrack block in the Main Fortress much as it might have looked in 1941

These were reserved for the Nazi guards. Initially the deportations came from the so-called Protectorate of Bohemia and Moravia (regions within Czechoslovakia) but later they came from Germany, Austria, the Netherlands, Denmark and Hungary. In the final months of the war prisoners arrived on evacuation transports and death marches from many other camps, as the Allies overran camps to the West and the East.

Initially the nearest railway station was some three or four miles away and the prisoners had to walk that distance with their pitiful collection of belongings under armed guard. However, one of the first projects they were set to work on, after the building of accommodation facilities, was a railway line into the camp, and from 1 June 1943 prisoners could be brought by rail right into a siding in the camp itself. In fact Ernst's brother Ludwig, also an inmate, was the chief engineer for the construction of this line. (His father's firm Ignatz Königsgarten had already constructed at least one previous railway line, from Hallstatt to Altaussee, at the turn of the century.) At one stage Ludwig managed to get a letter out of the camp in which he said how proud he was of what his team had achieved.

The railway line into the camp photographed in 2014, with its siding, constructed by a team of prisoners of which Ludwig was the chief engineer, and below, the same line on the day it was opened. Perhaps Ludwig is somewhere in the photo?

The fortress had been constructed as a garrison town and so the buildings consisted of three- or four-storey barrack blocks laid out on a grid system. There was a central open square with a church on one side. The barracks were designed to hold up to 6,000 troops. They were now made to accommodate at least 60,000 prisoners at any one time. Triple bunks were built in every room, and these were occupied two or three to a bed. Many were forced to sleep crammed into the attics, on the floorboards, or with no beds at all. There was minimal heating and minimal running water. There were cold showers once a week.

A typical bunk-room

The SS Camp Command had absolute power over the lives of the prisoners. Its members terrorised the inmates both psychologically and physically. Everyday lives were governed by an entire system of orders and prohibitions. Underneath the SS was a system of Jewish self-administration in charge of the internal functioning of the ghetto, but they were subject to the stringent demands and orders of the SS. Hunger caused the greatest single form of suffering for those in the ghetto, not only due to the insufficient volume of food, but also its monotony and lack of vitamins. Prisoners were made to work long hours in many locations, both within the ghetto and in work gangs outside. The transports, both into and out of the camp, were traumatising. From 1942 prisoners were taken away 'to the East' – no one really knew where. In fact they were taken to extermination camps (in particular Auschwitz) and labour camps in the occupied parts of Poland and the Soviet Union. All communication with the outside world was strictly controlled. All efforts were made to conceal the truth about life within the ghetto from the outside world; all mail was strictly censored and all attempts to thwart such controls were severely punished.

But Ernst did not have to endure these conditions long. He survived 41 days in the camp before he died on 15 January 1942. His death certificate states that his death took place at 3pm. Yes, there was a death certificate. So methodical were the Nazis that they even recorded the precise details of their most horrific crimes. By the end of the war the death rate may perhaps have made it impossible to produce such certificates, but in January 1942 a detailed death certificate was completed, signed and witnessed. The cause of death was stated by a doctor as meningitis. This became rife within the camp. It is an acute inflammation of the protective membranes covering the brain and the spinal cord. It is the result of viral or bacterial infection. Unless treated quickly its consequences are serious, and at that time usually fatal, as no adequate treatment was available. The death certificate gives his profession as *Sportlehrer* ('sports teacher'). It was probably thought best to give some profession. In his list of assets completed in 1938 he had described himself as *Privater* ('a man of independent means') but in the camp he probably thought it best to claim a profession.

News of his death did not of course reach the outside world or his family until after the war. Exactly when I am not sure, but information was made available by the International

Ernst's Death Certificate

Red Cross. My father, Lisi and Hugo would have learnt not only of Ernst's death but also of the other family members who had died. Ludwig, for example, Ernst's elder brother, had been deported to Theresienstadt not long after Ernst. He arrived there on 4 April 1942, aged 68, shortly after Ernst had died. Engaged, as he then was, in building the railway line, he survived there until 15 December 1943. By then the railway line had been completed and his skills were no longer required. Aged by then 70, he was transported again, this time for the final time, to Auschwitz Birkenau. There he did not survive. It is not known when he died – most probably the day he arrived.

All this must have been a shattering, even if anticipated, blow to Lisi, Hugo and my father. Yet never a word of this horror was mentioned to us as children nor did we pick any of it up. Yes, we learnt in our teens that Ernst was my father's father and that he had died in Theresienstadt, but nothing of the horror of it all was ever mentioned, and we were told that he had been sent there 'because he was anti-Hitler', and just that he had 'died there', as though that was (almost) the most natural thing in the world. It may sound naïve on our part, but we were never encouraged to enquire any further and did not do so.

This silence went hand-in-hand with another often expressed viewpoint, namely that Austria was a victim of Nazism and not one of its perpetrators. In this my parents were not alone. My father may have realised that this was not the whole truth, but I suspect my mother accepted it as fact. The view that Austria was the first victim of Nazism was one that not only suited Austria at the end of the war, but also one that suited the West as the Cold War began to take hold. It enabled the Western Allies to bring about an earlier end to the military occupation of Austria and in doing so encourage the Russians to end their occupation of Vienna and Eastern Austria. My mother in particular was always at pains to point out, if anyone was in any doubt, that my father was Austrian and not German, as though that automatically distanced him from any connection with the perpetrators of Nazi atrocities.

Chapter Seven: The 'Alpine Fortress'

It is time we turned our attention back to Altaussee. Ernst's house had been taken over and occupied by the Gestapo, but as the war finally drew to its inevitable conclusion, this small area of Austria played a much more significant role. It became a last refuge for many leading Nazis and was part of the mythical 'Alpine Fortress' where the Nazis would make their last stand. Long before the end of the war senior Nazis had recognised that the region around Altaussee was of particular strategic significance. In the Toplitzsee, a small lake at the end of the next valley, they not only set up an experimental base for launching an underwater rocket (a V3), but they also concealed forged UK banknotes that had been secretly manufactured by a group of concentration camp victims which were intended to be dropped from aircraft to destabilise England's economy. Both these valleys had the advantage that they backed onto a range of mountains known as the *Totes Gebirge* ('Dead Mountains') and access could therefore only be gained from one direction, namely the west. The region was therefore chosen by those Nazis who were determined to fight on in the face of defeat. Among them were Adolf Eichmann and Ernst Kaltenbrunner, Head of the Security Police and Security Services (the SS), which included the Gestapo. Eichmann already had his own house in the village; Kaltenbrunner set up his headquarters in a house which he requisitioned on the hillside above Altaussee known as the Villa Kerry. The owner Christl Kerry was an American Jewish artist who for some reason managed to remain 'protected' and who had agreed to move out and hand the house over to the Nazi leaders. It occupied an exceedingly good vantage point overlooking the whole valley.

As the war neared its end, many thousands of German and Austrian soldiers retreated towards Altaussee. The population of the region increased from its usual level of about 18,000 to a staggering 80,000. Not all were ardent Nazis. Many were war-weary soldiers, and if Gaiswinkler is to be believed, he and his group of resistance fighters succeeded by bravado and trickery in disarming many of them and using the weapons so obtained to build an ever-growing band of partisans. Others who had resisted conscription had been hiding in the mountains nearby for some time. It may not have been quite as simple as Gaiswinkler describes, but one of his group's achievements was to detect that the Nazi leaders in the Villa Kerry had buried a very substantial cache of gold and foreign currency in the garden of the villa, most of which his partisans succeeded in secretly removing. In the last days of the war they surrounded the house and arrested its occupants, handing them and the gold to the Americans when they arrived on 10 May. Gaiswinkler may well have exaggerated his role, but 60kg of buried Nazi gold was indeed recovered by the Americans from the Villa Kerry.

In addition to the gold, the SS records of the loot brought to Altaussee by Kaltenbrunner and hidden near the Villa Kerry or in the surrounding mountains, include:

2 million Swiss francs,

2 million American dollars,

50 crates, each of 50kg, of gold coins and gold objects,

5 crates of diamonds and other precious stones, and

a stamp collection with an estimated value of at least 5 million Goldmark.

Rather more macabrely, melted-down tooth gold from the concentration camps was also sent there by the German Reichsbank in the last days of the war.

However, although intended as an 'Alpine Fortress', when liberation came, two days after Germany surrendered, not a shot was fired. The region was taken over by an American officer with one tank, one jeep and five soldiers.

When Bridget and I visited Altaussee in 2011 we sought out the Villa Kerry. The house was empty at the time and we stood on the verandah where the Nazi leaders must have stood drinking their champagne and schnapps, and we admired the view. We looked carefully over the garden for any overlooked gold bullion or hard currency, but without luck! The house undoubtedly occupies a very impressive position.

The author on the terrace of the Villa Kerry, Kaltenbrunner's headquarters in April 1945

Kaltenbrunner himself, not surprisingly, was not amongst the Nazis to be captured in the Villa Kerry. The story of his capture and arrest, however, is not without interest. It is one that I first heard by chance when I visited Altaussee in 1997 with my mother and all our family. We were staying in the *Seehotel*, but we went and had dinner one night at the *Gasthof Loser* (where Bridget and I stayed in 2011 on our second visit) which was then owned by Herr Glaser. For some reason he told us about the capture of Kaltenbrunner. I may perhaps have asked him about walking to the *Appelhaus* in the mountains which my father had spoken of in my youth, and this may have elicited the story, as it was at the *Appelhaus* that Kaltenbrunner had been captured. He told me that the American officer who had led the group that captured him, had stayed at the *Gasthof Loser* many years later and given Herr Glaser a written account of the story, which he showed me. I asked him if I could borrow the document overnight. The next day I went into Bad Aussee and had it photocopied and returned the original to him. I still have this copy, but the story can also now be found on the Internet.

In brief, the story is this. A number of leading Nazis had been known to have retreated to the area around Altaussee. Several even had houses there, but Kaltenbrunner had a mistress there too. The Americans set out to track them down. Under questioning, the mistress gave away the fact that Kaltenbrunner and others had retreated to the *Appelhaus*, a mountain hut used by hunters and walkers, some four or five hours steep walk up into the *Totes Gebirge*. The American officer got a small patrol together, and shortly after midnight they set off up the track which starts from the end of the lake by the Seewiese. Although it was early May, there was still snow on the ground above a certain altitude and the going soon got tough. (When Bridget and I drove up to the *Loserhütte*, which is at the same altitude as the *Appelhaus*, in May 2011, we too were above the snowline – but there was no road in 1945!) But at around 5 a.m. they reached the hut and all was quiet. While some of the soldiers stood back with guns drawn, the officer calmly banged on the door. The occupants, awakened by the knocking, eventually opened the door. They were taken by surprise and they surrendered; but they had first taken the precaution of throwing some incriminating documents onto the smouldering fire. When questioned, they declined any knowledge of Kaltenbrunner, but the Americans noticed the smouldering embers of the fire and managed to retrieve the papers thrown onto it. The game was almost up.

The Germans were arrested and marched back down to Altaussee, arriving in the village about 11 a.m. As they came past the churchyard and then the *Seehotel*, Kaltenbrunner's mistress ran out from the small crowd that had gathered, rushed up to him and threw her arms around his neck crying "Ernst". Any lingering doubts as to his identity were now dispelled. Kaltenbrunner was taken into captivity and ended up amongst the leading Nazis tried at Nuremberg. He was ultimately found guilty of war crimes and hanged, along with others, in October 1946.

I was beginning to learn that Altaussee was not just a pretty summer holiday resort. Not only had the nearby Toplitzsee had been used for the development of a prototype V3 underwater rocket and to hide the forged UK banknotes, the local salt mine used to hide 6,500 works of stolen European art, but Kaltenbrunner had been dramatically captured there too. And he wasn't the only leading Nazi to either make his headquarters there at the end of the war or seek to hide there. Eichmann's wife had rented a house at Fischerndorf 8 in Altaussee before the war's end, and remained there until 1952. Eichmann himself was there for several days in early May 1945. (Kristl Kerry opened her door to him one night and promptly closed it again in his face, after which he vanished.) In the following years Eichmann again made several visits to Altaussee, not only to see his wife but also no doubt to retrieve the gold he had buried in the Bla-Alm, during which at least two attempts were made by Simon Wiesenthal in conjunction with the Austrian Police to arrest him, but he gave them the slip on both occasions. In 1951 Eichmann took the 'Odessa' route to South America, followed shortly afterwards by his wife, and it wasn't until May 1960 that Wiesenthal finally managed to track him down again, this time in Argentina, on which occasion the Israeli Secret Service swooped in, and, as might be suspected, with success. His trial in Jerusalem, covered dramatically by the world's press, was probably the trial of the century. The image of Eichmann in the witness box, behind a bullet-proof glass screen, is one of those images that remains with you for ever.

As for Altaussee, the Nazis and their supporters could not have remained there after the war without some degree of local help. For example, Frau Eichmann's post was censored by the occupying Allied forces, so sensitive items must have been sent via third parties. This could only have been achieved with the presence of Nazi sympathisers still in the area. The legacy of this would have continued to cause many divided loyalties for years to come. No wonder none of these things had been discussed with us as children, and it may also explain the feeling I always had of never knowing where local people's sympathies lay. It is comforting, however, now to know that the Frischmuth family, who had owned the *Seehotel* where we had stayed, were named by Gaiswinkler as loyal supporters of the Resistance movement. Frau Frischmuth, for example, had regularly taken food to the Resistance fighters hiding in the woods around the Villa Kerry.

Those then were some of the stories I had discovered about Altaussee, but more information about Ernst was to come to light as a result of another extraordinary coincidence, brought about once again by the re-erection of the plaque on the outside of the churchyard wall.

* * *

In the summer of 2013 another regular visitor to Altaussee, a writer named Carole Angier, whose family had always spent their summers there in the same rented house, was walking past the churchyard, and was struck by the sudden appearance of Ernst's plaque. The wording of it, it seemed to Carole, was quite a bold reminder of Austria's troubled past, and she was surprised. It also had a distinct relevance to an article she was writing about former Jewish residents of Altaussee. Knowing Ursula Kals-Friese, as she did, as the fount of all local knowledge, particularly where it concerned the Jewish community, she called in on her to find out what she knew about it. Ursula explained about me and my recent visits. But she noticed one other thing. She pointed out to Carole that my postcode in England was remarkably similar to Carole's. They both began with OX7. So when Carole returned home to England, she wrote me a postcard saying that she had seen the plaque and spoken to Ursula. I picked up the postcard and read it out to Bridget. The extraordinary thing was that Carole is also an old friend of Bridget's. So we immediately telephoned her and made a plan to meet.

Carole explained that she had been writing a short article on the Jewish community in Altaussee, and the story that Ursula told her intrigued her and fitted in to the theme of her article. According to Ursula the original plaque put up by my father had been smashed or removed on at least one occasion. Whether the plaque that I remember my father inspecting was the original or a replacement I do not know, but the fact that the present plaque had survived undamaged was to Carole a sign that Austria was finally coming to terms with its Nazi past.

Carole in turn put me in touch with Leo Walkner. Leo is an Austrian from Bad Aussee, a psychotherapist, who is doing a PhD in his late forties on the pre-war Jewish community of the Salzkammergut. We started exchanging emails. Leo was very glad to be in touch with a descendant of Ernst's, someone he had researched quite heavily for his thesis. In fact he knew much more about him than I did, and this was a real turning point in my research. I learnt for example not only that Ernst had built up an extensive art collection, but also that he had been a director of the Josefstadt Theatre in Vienna under Max Reinhardt in the 1920s. Leo had also established a number of contacts in the various Austrian archive offices, and he gave me all their email addresses. I followed them all up.

One of the first and most dramatic documents I came across was the *Vermögensverzeichnis* completed by Ernst in July 1938. This was a form required to be completed by all Jews pursuant to a law dated 27 April 1938, i.e. just over a month after the Anschluss. It required them, on pain of severe punishment, to provide details, including a monetary valuation, by 30 June of that year, of all assets, both real and personal, i.e. all property, bank accounts, investments and personal belongings. Ernst completed his, a few days late, on 4 July, and a copy of this is still in existence.

Opening section of the 'Vermögensverzeichnis'

His principal asset was the house in Altaussee, No.59 Fischerndorf, which he valued at 20-25,000 Reichsmarks. The form contains no details of any bank accounts or investments, but he may have already moved these out of Austria. He gives his nationality as Czech and the form, rather surprisingly, only requires him to give details of assets held within Austria. But under works of art he stated '18 oil paintings, copies of foreign masterpieces' and '1 silver cup' (no doubt a fencing trophy), but then, attached to the form is a typed inventory of some 200 items, broken down room by room. This list is divided into two sections, one headed '*Inventar der abzutransportierenden Gegenstände*', i.e. objects to be removed or transported, but by whom or to where was not specified, and the other, those objects not to be transported. It is also not clear whether this typed list was completed by Ernst or by some agent or official, but it seems more likely the latter.

But here suddenly was an insight into Ernst's life – a description, albeit brief and bland, of the furniture and objects that surrounded him, of the collections that he had accumulated. But did this list relate solely to Altaussee or to Vienna as well? The fact that it was broken down room by room would appear to indicate that it related to only one property, but the numbering of the items is very erratic which only adds to the confusion.

However, as a result of further documents obtained later and those seen by me on my visit to Vienna in 2014, it would seem as though the typed lists were done by officials of the *Bundesdenkmalamt*, tasked with the job of 'collecting and preserving' objects of national or local interest. (The *Bundesdenkmalamt* is the Austrian Federal Monuments Office and responsible for cultural heritage in Austria. Ironically it is also now responsible for the restitution of works of art looted by the Nazis – a sort of poacher turned gamekeeper.) The objects to be 'removed' or 'transported' were possibly those to be taken into 'safe-keeping' by the local museum, the *Heimathaus* in Bad Aussee, where many of them were put on display in 1941. What happened to them after that is still a matter of investigation, but some at least I know were returned to my father in 1949. I came across documentation to that effect on my visit to the *Bundesdenkmalamt* office in Vienna in May 2014, together with photographs of some of the items. Once again, quite amazingly, the card index, one for each item, of Ernst's entire collection is still available for inspection at the archive offices in Vienna!

I had in fact already come across evidence before my 2014 visit that my father had tracked down some of Ernst's belongings. In 2013 I had found on a US Army website (Fold3) a copy of a letter written by my father in August 1945 to an American Army colonel in which he states:

'...I have been able to recover most of the articles which had been kept at the Heimat Museum and where I am leaving them for the time being. I have been informed, however, that certain articles particularly vulnerable to bombing, e.g. some antique pottery belonging to me have been stored by the Heimat Museum in four cases in the salt mine. I am, naturally, anxious that these objects should be recovered as soon as possible and handed back to the Heimat Museum, the new curator of which, Herr Gielge, under the supervision of the newly appointed Regierungs Kommissär, Herr Gaiswinkler, looks after my property.'

He must have written this letter immediately after his visit to Altaussee on his trip from Hamburg to collect Hans Hotter. (The salt mine is of course the same salt mine in which many of Europe's stolen artworks were stored.)

A section of racking within the salt mine

But as to what actually happened to all these items next, I am still uncertain. I discovered evidence in Vienna that the four 'cases' ('*Kisten*') appear to have been retrieved from the salt mine, and the contents together with other items were handed over to a Dr. Branczik, as agent for my father, in August 1949. Dr. Branczik was a lawyer living in Altaussee (who coincidentally also came from Brno), but during the war he had been a prominent member of the National Socialist Lawyers' Association ('NSRB'), so one might think his credentials were suspect. But one must remember that it was virtually impossible to carry on a legal practice without signing up to the Nazi organisation, and Dr. Branczik is also on record as having acted for another Altaussee friend of Ernst's (Ernest Stiassni) in 1948 in trying to recover paintings of his that had also been seized. In any event my father clearly trusted him; but did my father ever fully recover all of Ernst's belongings or was he persuaded to leave some of them in the *Heimathaus*? In 2015 I visited the *Heimathaus* to see what I could discover, and the answer is I will probably never know. There are many items from that time still retained in the vaults of the museum, and any items of Ernst's that are still there were lumped together with those of Ernest Stiassni and one other, and there are no records to identify whose are whose. My father certainly got some of the furniture back, but as for all the 'objets' and paintings I do not know.

Chapter Eight: Central European Trip 2014

By the autumn of 2013 I had therefore, through reading and research, already built up a substantial picture of my family's movements and the life they had led or left behind. I had made contact with archivists in Brno, Berlin and Vienna. I had discovered addresses and dates. I had entered into detailed email correspondence with Leo Walkner and Carole Angier. Leo had sent me his doctorate thesis which included a long section on my grandfather. I had been in touch with the Dorotheum auction-house in Vienna, which had handled a lot of Nazi sales. Leo had put in hand further enquiries in the Altaussee region regarding Ernst's art collection. I had read numerous books describing life in Brno and Vienna leading up to the Second World War and detailing the lives of others who had fled the Nazis. All this had given me an insight into my father's family greater than anything I had previously known. But further investigations were still required. I needed to visit the archives both in Brno and Vienna - Brno because a lot of information online was only available in Czech, and Vienna because I felt there was more I could discover by a personal visit. I also wanted to visit the relevant places in the lives of those concerned. I had discovered that the old Königsgarten home in Brno, 55 Dornych, was still standing, although it was about to be pulled own for redevelopment and may even have already been condemned. So a visit to Brno was high on the list. It would also mean I could visit the Tugendhat villa (the subject of *The Glass Room* by Simon Mawer), which has now been restored and is open to the public. I also wanted to visit Theresienstadt where Ernst had died. I also hoped I might visit Bratislava where my father had briefly worked in 1936. And I wanted to find the apartments where Ernst and Lisi had lived in Vienna.

So I teamed up with an old friend, Mark Holland, and after a winter of planning we set out for Prague on 8 May 2014.

Mark had booked us into an old monastery a little way out from the centre, part of which was now run as a hotel, but this gave us a chance to enjoy the trams which are so much a part of the character of the city. There were old trams which hadn't changed for years and modern ones in the form of bendy-trams, but they all had the same old familiar clang to their bells. The next day dawned bright and sunny, and we spent the day exploring the city, with its many bridges, its huge castle complex and its attractive old town.

On the Saturday we set off early to Theresienstadt, a journey of some 40 miles. We had decided against taking an organised tour from Prague, and preferred instead to find our own way by public transport and determine our own timetable. Given the language difficulties and the lack of any helpful signs it was not quite as easy as we had thought to find the right bus, or even the right bus stop, but we managed it. The journey was about an hour, and we found ourselves disembarking in Theresienstadt about 500 yards from the main entrance gate to the Small Fortress. Between us and the gate was a huge memorial ground with rows and rows of numbered headstones. It was a sombre moment. We walked slowly the length of the memorial ground, across the bridge over the moat, and through the black and white striped arch of the stone entrance tunnel so reminiscent of Nazi prisons.

We signed up for a tour of the fortress. We visited rows and rows of solitary confinement cells, we visited the barrack blocks where prisoners were crammed three to a bed on triple-tiered bunks some 60 people to a room, with one loo, one basin and one small stove. We saw the shower rooms and the punishment rooms, we saw the bell which was rung for the interminable roll-calls, we saw the firing-squad wall and the gallows, and we saw miles and miles of narrow tunnels with slit openings which formed part of the original defences for which purpose the fortress had been built. What we saw and what we heard was quite horrific, but I remained reasonably confident that Ernst had not been amongst the prisoners in the

Small Fortress, which was used mainly for criminals and as a punishment block. Nevertheless it was an emotional and humbling experience, and one during which none of the visitors spoke very much.

We then walked on to the Main Fortress. This was a 10 to 15-minute walk away and as we approached through its main entrance tunnel I realised I was walking into the camp where Ernst had ended his days. I felt that one of the goals of my trip was about to be achieved.

The Main Fortress is the old (fortress) town originally built in the late eighteenth century. There was a museum building (the old school) but it did not contain anything of great interest. What I wanted to do was get a feel for the whole camp, a measure of its size and layout, and a feel for how the prisoners were housed. I also wanted to see the railway siding that Ludwig had constructed, and the cemetery. But first we needed some lunch. There was but one shop, a dingy general purpose and food store, very basic, but we managed to obtain the ingredients for some kind of a sandwich, a yoghurt and a fizzy drink. We took it across the road to a bench, broken but just serviceable, on the edge of the grass square in the middle of the town. This was the square the prisoners had not been allowed to walk on. The church was on one side, and barrack blocks or smaller buildings along the others. I imagined Ernst, in mid-winter, making his way around the outside of this square, perhaps being allowed into the church, perhaps waiting for one of the endless roll-calls, perhaps just getting some fresh air, or trying to find firewood for the stove, perhaps in a working party, or perhaps too ill to work.

We visited one of the barrack blocks in which a room had been re-created as it would have been during the war. There were old coats and other items of clothing hanging over the ends of the bunks, all with yellow stars of David sewn on to them, makeshift washing lines, old shoes and other items. The

The square in the middle of Theresienstadt (in 2014), which was forbidden to the prisoners, with the church on one side, where Mark and I sat for our meagre lunch

room was grossly overcrowded but conveyed a sense of great comradeship and a certain spirit of defiance.

We walked on to where the railway line had been built into the camp. This was the line for which Ludwig was the chief engineer. I thought that even if Ernst had died before this project had got underway, Max would more than likely have been involved in its construction as well as Ludwig. Max had died of tuberculosis on 23 July 1943, and so would have witnessed the opening of the line and the arrival of the first train into the camp on 1 June of that year. How many hours, I wondered, had they sweated away in its construction?

We walked on and towards the crematorium and the large memorial cemetery. This was laid out with lots of small plain marble 'headstones'. I laid a piece of rosemary Bridget had given me on one of these unmarked blocks, and bid farewell to Ernst. Mark joined me, we took some photos and walked slowly back to the main square and waited for our bus back to Prague.

A preserved bunk-room in Theresienstadt

The next day we spent further sightseeing in Prague. Some of it I had seen before when I visited Prague in 1991, but I particularly wanted to revisit one of the small Jewish synagogues where I remembered a very moving exhibition of drawings done by Jewish children while in captivity in concentration camps. Most of the children did not of course survive, but by some extraordinary irony of fate their drawings did. I tracked down the synagogue in question which is called the Pinkas Synagogue. The exhibition of children's drawings was still there in an upstairs room, but the synagogue had been renovated since I was last there and is now dedicated to the 80,000 Jewish victims of the Holocaust from Bohemia and Moravia, and their names – yes, all of them, complete with dates of birth and death – are inscribed on the walls inside the synagogue in a bold and semi-Hebraic script. They are listed alphabetically according to the town from where they were deported, so it was not difficult to find the right area of wall, but they reach from floor to ceiling and so many of the names would have been hard to see. I couldn't believe my luck therefore when I saw Ernst's name on the wall of the first entrance room I came into, at about shoulder height, and so readable without any difficulty. This was another very moving moment.

The author in the memorial cemetery, with the crematorium in the background (far left)

The next day, Monday, we took the train to Brno, where our hotel, located very conveniently across the road from the station, turned out to be very comfortable too. I had visited Brno about two years before, but we had not had much time then to explore the town itself (we had been based there for a tour of Moravian country houses and gardens) and anyway at that time my family research had not really got underway. Also, the Tugendhat villa had been closed for renovation. But it was now open again, and we had pre-booked a tour (essential) for 3 p.m. the next afternoon. The other essential things on my to-do-list were to visit the Jewish cemetery, find the old family home, and visit my contact in the Brno city archives.

The Jewish cemetery was easily reached by tram from the station. I had looked it up online before I left England, so I recognized the stop to get off at (just as well as most of the names everywhere are in Czech, including the bus stops!).

The section of wall in the Pinkas Synagogue containing Ernst's name and dates (Ernst becomes translated as Arnost in Czech)

There are formal gates and a small entrance building and one pays a small fee to enter; so it is clearly looked after and cared for, but do not expect the mown lawns and tidy graves we are used to. There is no grass, as huge trees shroud everything, and the graves, heavily covered in ivy, are closely packed beneath them. The headstones and ornate tombs are all huge. It is like a scene from Dickens. But a map is available (online and at the gate) showing the position of each grave, and each row and block is clearly numbered. So it didn't take me long to find the graves of all the Königsgartens on my list, together with a few Brücks and Jellineks as well. I had the place virtually to myself. Because of the huge trees and wildly growing ivy, it is quite dark, and one could be anywhere. There is no sense of being in the middle of a city. You feel as though you are walking through the ghosts of your ancestors and transported back in time, at least to the 19th century, to a world of horse-drawn carriages and candles. The opening scene of Great Expectations comes to mind, and you expect to see a shackled criminal appear from the gloom, demanding food and the release of his chains. But it was a very moving moment for me. Here, gathered together, were more family members than I had ever seen together alive.

As previously mentioned 55 Dornych was the family home. The factory had long gone, but thanks to Google Streetview I had managed to establish that the house was still standing (or had been recently), even if rather run-down. In fact the whole area looked rather neglected and I gathered that the house was about to be pulled down and the area re-developed. So I hastened there on another tram hoping I was in time to find the house still standing. I was. At first sight it looked empty. The ground floor windows were half boarded up and there was no sign of life. But while I was photographing it I saw someone emerge from the front door. I went over and rang the bell. There was no answer, so I walked round to the back. There was a rather rickety-looking old wooden verandah at first-floor level, which could once have been rather grand, and the house was L-shaped, so even larger than it seemed from the front. There was a back door with another bell. I tried that and a woman came to the door.

Königsgarten tombs in the Brno cemetery

We got by with a bit of German, and I established that the ground floor was now used as a warehouse where she obviously worked. To get into the rest of the house I would need to try the front door again. So I returned to the front and rang the bell several times. Eventually another woman put her head out of an upstairs window, but she did not want to come down and open the door, nor did she speak any German. Eventually the man whom I had seen leaving, returned and opened the door, after which she too came down to the hall. I tried to explain that this had been my grandfather's house, and that I hoped I could see inside. Perhaps they feared that I was going to try and evict them – they seemed more like squatters – and they were very reluctant to let me inside, but eventually they gave in, and I followed them through a hallway to a stone staircase at the far end, and up to the first floor. They did not let me in to the door of their flat, but there were about ten pairs of shoes on the landing outside and I could hear several voices inside, so I thought it best not to press my request. If I were not to emerge from the building, it could be some time before anyone was able to trace me! (Mark was off sightseeing and did not know any details of where I had gone!). The flight of stone steps to the top floor was cordoned off; the banisters had gone and it looked decidedly precarious. So I could not venture any further.

So that was my grandfather's house, and almost certainly where my father had been born. It had been divided up in such a way that it was hard to tell what it had originally looked like inside, but it must have had a fair number of rooms, and quite probably some large ones. I call it my grandfather's house, but it was of course originally my great-grandfather Ignatz's house. It had housed him and his family, it was where his eldest son Fritz and Lisi had lived, where Fritz had died, where Ernst came to stay, and where Hugo and almost certainly my father were born. Why had I never asked my father more about his family home? Why did my father never talk about it? But I had found it, even got inside, and it was thrilling. I got the tram back to the hotel feeling very happy. I had achieved more than I had expected.

The first task the next morning was to visit my contact in the City Archives. These were a little way out of the centre and I thought it wise to take a taxi. When I got there I was glad that I had done so. I might never have found it otherwise. For some months or more I had been in touch with a Dr. Bohumir Smutny. He had responded to one of my Internet enquiries and we had entered into email correspondence in German. (His first language was of course Czech.) He had told me that he had put together a 'register' of Brno industrialists, which included my great-grandfather Ignatz, and I was quietly thrilled and encouraged that Ignatz had been identified and included. I didn't know whether a meeting would be at all productive, but I felt I had to see his 'Register'.

55 Dornych, Brno – the family home (as photographed by the author in 2014)

I phoned ahead and he was expecting me. The archives were in a modern building in a kind of Business Park, and he took me to a meeting room on the fourth floor with a large boardroom-type table and plate glass windows. There on the table was a huge A3-size bound hardback volume, at least two inches thick, which was entirely his creation. When I asked him what had led to him producing it, he merely replied that he had been interested in the idea and had been given leave to do so. A page was flagged, and what immediately caught my eye was a

'Ignatz Königsgarten' – *the company letterhead, showing the family house alongside the factory*

drawing, taken I imagine from the company's letterhead, showing the factory at 55 Dornych and Ignatz's family house beside it, just as I had seen it the day before. Below it was an article, written by Dr. Smutny, about the factory and the family business. It was of course all in Czech so I couldn't understand it, and Dr. Smutny's German was not quite good enough for him to translate it all for me, but he did his best. I couldn't believe someone had done so much detailed research on so many Jewish businesses in Brno. My father, who never returned to Brno in his later life, would have been amazed.

Another large volume lay on the table beside it and again a page was flagged. It was an old photograph album of all Brno's leading industrialists and there on one of the pages was a photo of Fritz. Many of those photographed were of course Jewish, but many were not. It was extraordinary to see these two great books treating all these industrialists equally. For the first time no mention was made of race or religion. Perhaps, I felt, the prejudices of the past were now finally buried, or at least in this small corner of the Czech Republic.

We talked on about Ignatz and my family, during the course of which Dr. Smutny mentioned the existence of a file. Never for a moment imagining it would be easily retrievable (I was leaving Brno the following morning) I asked whether it would be possible for me to see it. "I think so," he said, and disappeared down the corridor. Within ten minutes he was back bearing a file relating to the company 'Ig. Königsgarten'. Fortunately the file was in German! I delved into it.

The file started with a *Protokoll* recording the founding of the company in 1887, and then in 1914 ownership passing to Ignatz's second son Ludwig and his wife Helene (the parents incidentally of Gerda[4], a cousin of my father's whom I remember quite well, who survived the war and lived in Paris). Fritz, the eldest son, it will be remembered, who was the first husband of my grandmother Lisi, had died in 1908. Helene incidentally also died young, at the age of 29, in October 1918, after a short illness. (She is buried in the Jewish cemetery in Brno.) But things start to get more sinister in 1940. Dated 20 February 1940 there is a document with the heading 'Appointment of a Trustee for the Jewish firm Ig. Königsgarten'

---

[4] When I was researching this book I wrongly assumed Gerda had long-since died, since my mother had not mentioned her for many years, although I was unable to trace any records of her death. However in 2016 I discovered by chance that she had only died in November 2013, aged 101, and had been living in Paris until her death. My account of tracking down her neighbour and next-of-kin and her survival throughout the war is contained in Appendix IV.

which records the appointment of Engineer Josef (not such an Aryan name!) Malnatti as 'Trustee' of the company in accordance with the law of 21 June 1939 concerning Jewish property. A further document dated 16 December 1941, under the heading 'Aryanisation of the firm of Ig. Königsgarten', records the outright sale of the business to the rival metal company. So the business was taken away from him. This was in fact the beginning of the end. Not long after that, on 4 April 1942, Ludwig too was deported to Theresienstadt.

How long the factory survived I do not know, but today it has gone. Only the house remains, and that too will probably have gone before any one of us visits Brno again. But my visit to Dr. Smutny was immensely worthwhile. His large books and his file had resurrected a bit of a past age, in which the name Königsgarten flourished and thrived at the centre of Brno's commercial and industrial life.

I took a bus back into town. On the streets and on the buses few people speak English or German, and when away from any tourist venues it is very easy to feel one is in a far-away and unfamiliar land. Perhaps Chamberlain had been right to describe Czechoslovakia as a 'far-away country of which we know nothing'.

The Tugendhat villa, which we visited that afternoon, is really fascinating, not only for its architectural significance, but for anyone who has read *The Glass Room* by Simon Mawer, for its historical significance too. The house was designed by Mies van der Rohe for the Tugendhat family in 1929 and was revolutionary for its time. Its two most remarkable features are the green onyx wall at the back of the open-plan sitting room which catches the full rays of the setting sun and then becomes transparent, and the large plate glass windows opposite it which can be lowered right down to floor level. They disappear into the basement below, where they are controlled by hefty electrical winding-gear. But the design of the house and furniture is ultra-minimalist, and the bedrooms in particular look far from comfortable!

The Tugendhat Villa in Brno, as seen from the road

Mark Holland in the garden

The green onyx wall

The historical significance is that the Tugendhats were forced to flee from here after the arrival of the Nazis. The SS then took the house over and used it for so-called 'medical' purposes, namely the gruesome analysis and measurement of Jewish heads and other features to lay down a definitive blueprint for identifying members of that race. It was used for this purpose throughout the war, after which it fell into Soviet hands and was used, quite inappropriately, as an army barracks. By 1989, when communism fell, it had, needless to say, been much ruined, and was only recently restored to its original glory, and finally opened to the public in 2013. It is well worth a visit for its architecture alone.

* * *

The next morning we took the train to Bratislava. This had been an important city in Czechoslovakia between the wars and is only some 70 kms. from Vienna. It is now the capital of Slovakia and we had been invited to dinner by the Spanish ambassador, to whom we had been given an introduction by a mutual friend. But my real reason for wanting to visit the city is because my father had briefly worked there in 1936, after leaving Paris and accepting a job with the 'Syndicate of the Slovakian Sugar Industry'. Why he accepted this job or what exactly it was I will probably never know. All my father had ever said was that he had got a job briefly in Czechoslovakia and I had assumed it was in banking and probably in Prague. Perhaps the 'Syndicate' had been a client of his Paris bank or he wanted to rediscover his home country? Who knows? But in any event it was not long before he was scooped up again by another merchant bank in London and returned to England. But I was intrigued just to walk in his footsteps and discover just a bit about this not-much-visited capital. And anyway it was on our way to Budapest and we had an interesting-sounding invitation to dinner!

There is not a lot to write about Bratislava. It is on the Danube and has a typical mediaeval old town centre, a grand opera house, a few large squares and many narrow streets. But outside the immediate centre it has grown in a dull tasteless fashion in true Soviet style. In fact even on the edge of the old city the Soviets had little regard for historical buildings, having built a huge suspension bridge across the river with a dual-carriageway approach road running right past and above the main door of the cathedral!

We had an enjoyable dinner with the ambassador and his wife and continued our journey the next day by train towards Budapest. We left the train at a small town on the Danube called Esztergom, a former mediaeval capital of Hungary, from where we took a boat to Visegrad (another old capital). I felt we could not travel through that part of Europe without doing at least a small stretch by boat. From there we took a bus to Szentendre, once an artists' village but now rather touristy, where we spent the night. The following day we took the local train into Budapest and had two interesting days of sightseeing, including sampling one of the many open-air baths with natural hot springs, a concert and some excellent restaurants.

On Sunday evening, after nearly three days in Budapest, Mark and I parted. He returned to England, and I took an intercity train to Vienna – very fast, very comfortable, a three-hour journey and only 29 euros First Class! Why can't we do the same in England?

* * *

In Vienna I was extremely lucky to be able to stay with Mark and Camilla Macdonnell. Camilla is Bridget's sister-in-law – technically her half-sister-in-law. (Camilla was Andrew's much younger half-sister, being the daughter of his father by his father's second marriage.) Camilla's mother is German, so she is bilingual and therefore completely at home with the language. Mark works for the Dorotheum, Vienna's leading auction house, where he is a specialist in Italian Old Masters. They have three delightful children, ranging in age from about seven to four. I had the best part of five days ahead of me to pursue my enquiries and research.

My programme started first thing on the Monday morning. I was due to meet Leo Walkner outside the Hofburg at 9 o'clock. (Leo Walkner, it will be remembered, was my Austrian contact who was doing a PhD on Jewish families in and around Altaussee.) The Hofburg is not just home to the Imperial Palace and the Spanish Riding School, but also more mundanely to the *Bundesdenkmalamt*. This is the Viennese office responsible for the country's cultural heritage, and which has amongst its many records the files of those Jews whose assets had been seized by the Nazis. Ernst's file is amongst them. I had been in touch with Leo for some time, and through him I had already obtained copies of several significant documents from the *Bundesdenkmalamt*, but Leo had now arranged for us to meet a Frau Schallmeiner in their office at 9 a.m. on that Monday morning.

This was a much awaited visit, as I already knew something of the records we could see. But as we mounted the stairs something more mundane was on my mind – namely a cup of coffee! I had rather assumed we would be offered a coffee on arrival, but no such luck! Frau Schallmeiner was incredibly willing and helpful, but coffee or refreshments were obviously not something on her agenda, even though we were there nearly three hours! It was down to business straight away!

As previously mentioned, on 27 April 1938, just over a month after the Anschluss, the Nazis had passed a law in Austria requiring all Jews to complete a detailed form listing all their assets, both real and personal, i.e. land, buildings, bank accounts and shares, as well as personal belongings, namely furniture, art, jewellery and other valuables. The form was called *Verzeichnis über das Vermögen von Juden* ('Register of Jewish property') and was required to be completed by 30 June 1938, failing which heavy penalties were spelt out, including fines, imprisonment and confiscation. Ernst and Max had both completed one of these forms and I had been able to obtain copies of these from the *Bundesdenkmalamt* several months before. In Ernst's case the form was accompanied by a separate typed list covering some ten pages detailing all his furniture, paintings, pottery and other artistic or cultural items. The form also recorded that he owned the villa in Altaussee; his flat in Vienna one must assume to have been rented.

One of the questions that I hoped to establish on my visit to the *Bundesdenkmalamt* was whether the list of items related solely to his house in Altaussee or the flat in Vienna or both, and if possible what happened to the items. The house in Altaussee I knew had been requisitioned by the Gestapo, but it was not clear what eventually happened to all its contents. I knew that when Miss Schiff died in 1974, the auction of its contents included many items of my grandfather's, so some at least must have been recovered by my father. (Ursula had even bought three of them – one of them, the porcelain tile, now being in Tessa's house in France.) I knew nothing about the flat in Vienna except its address.

In all I made two visits to the *Denkmalamt* during my week in Vienna, and although I wasn't able to find answers to all my questions at that time, much progress was made. Matters were made more complicated by the fact that many of Ernst's belongings were collected and stored together with those of two other Jewish families and friends of Ernst's, who also had houses in Altaussee, namely the Stiassnys and the Mautners. Although the many lists were intended to identify the owners of each item, it made it much more difficult to keep track of them. But an index card had also been completed for each item, some amazingly even with photographs attached, and these records are all still intact. They enabled me to identify, for example, a large carved oak chest which had been there at the time of Miss Schiff's death as being one of my grandfather's items, as it also featured in a photograph given to me by Ursula taken at the time of the auction.

One of the questions which continued to puzzle us all, as Leo and I pursued our enquiries, was whether the items listed in Ernst's *Vermögensverzeichnis* and its attached list all related to Altaussee, as seemed to be the case, or not. In which case, why had he not disclosed any of the contents of his Vienna flat? I still do not have a complete answer to this, but one of the more amazing documents produced by Frau Schallmeiner was an export permit granted to Ernst on 5 October 1938, allowing him to export certain items (two oil paintings and six engravings) from Vienna to Brno. The document bears a Customs stamp indicating that they crossed the border into Czechoslovakia on 1 December 1938.

Elated by this find, I asked Frau Schallmeiner to check whether any similar export permit existed for Lisi, and lo and behold, one was found. Hers was dated 10 August 1938, which ties in with the date of her departure to London and relates to 23 (unnamed) items. Although it doesn't give the ultimate destination of the goods, the customs stamp shows that the goods crossed the frontier into Germany at Passau, which is in the right direction for England and the Channel ports. Ernst's

The interior of the Villa Königsgarten at the time of the auction, showing some of Ernst's furniture

permit relates only to eight items, presumably from his flat in Vienna, and what happened to the rest of his belongings is of course unknown. Whether the rest were not valuable enough to require an export licence, or whether he was not allowed or did not ask to take more is not known. That these documents still exist seems to me quite amazing.

Leo and I also visited another of the State Archive offices during my visit to Vienna. But further enquiries still need to be made in Linz and Bad Aussee, and these are in hand. It does however seem clear that most, if not all, the contents of Ernst's villa in Altaussee were moved first of all to the *Heimathaus* museum in Bad Aussee and then some of them were moved again for safe keeping in four crates into the salt mine. It seems that my father retrieved (in name at least, if not physically) the contents that were retained by the *Heimathaus*, and that he eventually obtained the release of the four crates. He may not have ever got them all back physically, but I could find no evidence that any of his belongings had either been sold off or found their way into (private) Nazi hands, but that is not to say that did not happen. What the contents of his Vienna apartment were exactly, and what happened to them, is still for the most part a mystery.

Finally, I unearthed a letter from my uncle Hugo indicating that he had lived in No. 17 Prinz Eugen Strasse until 13 March 1938, the day after the Anschluss. Both the date and the location tied in absolutely with the 'novella' that my grandmother Lisi had written entitled *Last Days in Vienna* (see Appendix I) which indicated even more clearly that this appeared to be a story more of fact than of fiction. My family's past was coming to life.

What, however, really brought it to life was the next episode of my stay in Vienna. I wanted to visit the flats where Ernst, Max and Lisi had lived and to try and get a feel for their life there. I had discovered the addresses from the records available online and I knew they were all close to each other and all centred around the Wohllebengasse. This was the street which gave its name to the book *Good Living Street*, by Tim Bonyhady, which describes so well life in *fin de siècle* Vienna and leading up to the events of 1938. What I had not expected was the stunning position of Ernst's flat in No.2 Argentinierstrasse, nor that I would be able to get beyond the front door.

On a sunny afternoon I walked across town to find it. No.2 Argentinierstrasse is on the corner of the Karlsplatz, right opposite the impressive Karlskirche with its two distinctive tall towers. Being on the corner, it could not have been in a better position, giving views in two directions, over the square and towards the church. From its location I could see that any flat there was going to be bright and spacious. I knew that Ernst's flat was No.5 on the 1st Floor. I was bold and rang the bell on the building's front door, but there was no answer. However, it appeared that there was a small travel agency office at the back of the ground floor and from time to time staff came in and out. On one occasion I bluffed my way in as they opened the door, and made my way to the first floor. There I was, staring at Ernst's old front door. Like everything in the building it looked original, and well maintained. The lift, which was situated in the central well of the three-sided stone staircase, was typical of early 20th century lifts, built of glass and polished wood, with a leather bench seat, a brass grille door and a brass control panel, and itself contained in wrought-iron work running from top to bottom of the stairwell. It even had a brass plate with the name of the manufacturer and the date '1908'. So this would have been the lift used by Ernst. I travelled up to the top floor and down again in it, just for the ride.

I tried the inside doorbell to flat No.5, but again there was no answer. However, I took the name of the occupant and thought I would try to ring. However a couple of days later I returned with Leo, who was also intrigued to see the flat and its location. Again there was no answer from the outside doorbell, but I knew how to get in! We waited for someone to be let in to the travel agency and slipped in behind them, making our excuses. Emboldened by our actions so far, I thought I would try to speak to a neighbour, and as luck would have it I could see and hear signs of life in the flat immediately above Ernst's. This would be absolutely perfect as the flat would (presumably) be identical in shape to his. I rang the bell and a lady answered. As soon as we explained the reason for our visit she could not have been more welcoming, and invited us in. She sat us down in a splendid drawing room and we told her our story. She herself was Hungarian by birth, in her late '70s or early '80s, and had lived in America for some years, but had now been living in this flat for almost fifty years. She spoke very good English and knew all about the history of the building. She knew the woman who lived in Ernst's flat and said she was away on holiday in Italy for two weeks, and that she had inherited not just the flat but the whole building from her uncle when he died. So her uncle might even have been Ernst's landlord!

The door to Ernst's flat, No.5, on the 1st Floor of No.2 Argentinierstrasse

The flat we were in was furnished in a style that I felt could have been Ernst's, so typical was it of that generation. But the main thing was the layout of the flat itself and the views. The main reception rooms ran round the corner of the building and were all inter-connected with grand double doors. A corridor ran along the inside. The views from the principal rooms were magnificent, and the windows, architraves, cornices and door-panelling were all full of character. There was a parquet floor throughout. I felt I had stepped back in time and had entered Ernst's life. It was a thrilling moment. (A photograph of the interior appears on the front cover of this book.)

After we left, we walked around the neighbourhood, visiting each of the buildings where Lisi had lived in Schwindgasse and Wohllebengasse, and finally, round the corner again to Hugo's flat in Prinz Eugen Strasse. The building was now the Monaco Embassy, but it was quite clear that any young man's flat (probably on a top floor) would have had a splendid view over the wall opposite into the gardens of the Belvedere Palace (just as described by Lisi in her 'novel').

I couldn't help pondering again how nothing had been said about Ernst when I had first visited Vienna with my parents in August 1963 (the year of the Great Train Robbery, which I remember reading about in the newspapers while we were in Altaussee), and we had visited the Belvedere and walked across the Schwarzenberg Platz – I remember the Russian tank still standing there at that time. We had been so close to where Ernst had lived and yet my father had not taken us there nor, as far as I know, visited it himself, at least not on that occasion. All he ever said was that his mother used to live near the Schwarzenberg Platz, when once I had asked him.

In between my visits to the various archives and wandering the streets around the Belvedere, I of course took the opportunity to see all the various Klimts on display in Vienna. These were spread between the Belvedere, the Leopold Museum and the Secession Building, the latter housing the famous 'Beethoven Frieze' – so called because a statue of Beethoven originally formed the centerpiece for this huge mural. I tried to absorb as much of that era as I could.

***

Finally, there was one last excitement. I visited the Dorotheum on more than one occasion, not just because my host Mark Macdonnell worked there, but also because I had been in touch with a Katja Fischer, who worked in their Provenance Department. I had previously written to enquire whether the Dorotheum might have auctioned any of Ernst's artworks – they were an established outlet for items seized by the Nazis. She had responded to my enquiry, but their sales catalogues for that period were not such as to make any search of that nature very easy. We met for a coffee and a lively chat in their splendid café and she quizzed me all about my family's past and its connections. I was very touched that she seemed so genuinely interested, but she explained that this was all relevant to her understanding of the provenance of so many works of art of that period. However, and this was the big

*Klimt's Adele Bloch-Bauer I (1907)
and the Belvedere Palace where it hung until recovered
by Maria Altmann in 2006*

surprise, it so happened that on the coming Thursday evening at 6 p.m. there was an auction of modern art, and there were no less than four Klimt drawings being auctioned, one of them an early preparatory drawing of Adele Bloch-Bauer done in 1903. They were of course all on display, and I went to look at them. The drawing of Adele was so obviously a Klimt, more so than any of his others. I became very excited and felt I couldn't resist the opportunity to try and acquire such an item! But there was the small question of the price! The reserve was 24,000 euros. I had a couple of days to think about it.

  Not surprisingly the idea of attending an auction with a particular interest in mind was thrilling, and so at 6 p.m. on the Thursday I found myself sitting in the auction room lapping up the champagne that was being plentifully handed round and perusing the catalogue. The Klimts were near the beginning of the auction, so I didn't have long to wait. The bidding started at 16,000 euros. I thought I would not show my hand too soon, so I waited. At 20,000 I raised my little paddle. A counter bid was put in at 22,000. I raised my paddle again – 24,000. But I had decided beforehand that that would be my limit and I stuck to it. The bidding continued until it was finally sold for 36,000. I felt I had made the right decision. I was not able to discover who the buyer was – their names are kept secret. But that had provided an unexpected and rather exciting finale to my trip.

  The following day, after a brief visit to the Leopold Museum and a final look at some more Klimts, I caught the plane home to England. I felt I had achieved almost all I could have hoped for. Since returning home there have been a number of enquiries still to pursue, and these continue, but for the most part I feel I have uncovered a small part of a dark period of history that engulfed my father's family and which it was too painful for him to discuss during his lifetime. Whether he ever thought that I would be able to piece together something from the few items left in the attic of his house, I shall never know. Since he died before the invention of the Internet, he could never have imagined the extent to which this has been possible.

It has in any event been a moving experience for me, and one that I have felt driven to pursue since the moment I started. The timing is also rather extraordinary, in that a number of the events described in this account have been made into films during the course of the writing of this book, and so these matters have been brought to the public's attention to a degree that only such media can achieve. But maybe that is how it should be. These events may just have been too painful for my father to discuss with his children when they were young, and by the time we were grown up perhaps he thought that bygones were best left as bygones. I shall never know

Appendix I: Last Days in Vienna

by Lisi Bohne-Königsgarten

"Enough for today" said Benno. He stood at the window and looked out. It was the afternoon of 14 March 1938. A pale sky framed the familiar picture. Below the old wall along the edge of the dark mountain range, trees that as yet had no leaves, but delicate twigs giving a hint of the coming spring; while behind was a pair of slender towers and the beautiful dome with its green patina. On the right hand side the matt coloured front of the Belvedere Castle. On the street below children played and on a corner a street organ played *The Blue Danube*.

Benno saw and heard it all; yes, he saw and heard with heightened clarity. But nevertheless he felt the presence of the girl acutely. As always Luise sat in front of the typewriter. Benno was working on his book, *The Early Classical Age*, and she had been his secretary for six months. All he knew about her was that her name was Luise von Bruckner; that she came from an old Austrian officer's family; that she was an orphan and that she lived with her aunt, the widow of a civil servant. She had proved to be conscientious, intelligent and tactful; he could not wish for a more suitable secretary. Sometimes though she seemed to him to be too quiet, too introspective, almost shy.

When he was dictating, all he saw was the blonde parting of her hair as she bent over the typewriter and her slender fingers flying over the keys; when he paused she raised her pure white face and faun-brown eyes to look at him. But never a question, never a word of praise. Was it a lack of interest in his work? He would so like to have heard some words of encouragement from her beautiful mouth. He found it remarkable that the opinion of this exquisite but aloof creature meant so much to him. He was almost offended by her reticence, but her simple presence did him good, it exhilarated him and made him creative. The atmosphere in the room was friendlier when she was there and when she went everything sank into a monotonous grey. Today the pauses in his dictation became longer and longer, his mind wandered and he kept losing his train of thought. What was the point of writing such a book in days like these – *The Early Classical Age* – and Hitler! All of a sudden it seemed to him to be unimportant and alien. Descriptions of ancient Greece only emphasised the evil of the present world. It was pointless. "Enough!" he said again and turned to the girl. "It is no good."

"Perhaps after a little break?" he heard her murmur. "There really is no hurry" he said in a tired voice. He hoped she would encourage him to continue, but Luise simply stood up and walked to the mirror to put on her hat. From where he stood Benno could see both the girl and himself in the mirror; Luise, slender and long legged, a small head on delicate shoulders. Her silver blonde hair flowed out from under the small hat and her faun-brown eyes shone in her pale white face. He was not much taller than she was, but his broad shoulders emphasised his masculinity. His dark face and straight dark hair were in contrast to the pale creature beside him. Adam and Eve – man and wife – his thoughts ran wild. Nonsense – ridiculous! His family came from the north; his great-grandparents had come from Spain and he had inherited the hot blood and dark complexion of those who grew up under the burning Spanish sun.

Benno helped Luise into her coat and the perfume of her hair filled his nostrils as he touched her slender shoulders. As she gave him her hand and looked up at him she said in a gentle voice full of encouragement, "Things are really not so bad Doctor. You shouldn't worry so much." And then, "You really don't look well Doctor."

He was silent thinking that of course, how could she understand his fear? – she was Aryan – nothing bad would happen to her whatever happened in Austria – and it was good that she was safe! But how empty the room would be when she left and how slowly the hours would pass until the next day. He heard himself say "Luise, are you perhaps free this evening?" She answered at once, "Oh yes, I am almost always free in the evenings." The answer came so quickly that it was almost as if she had been waiting for the question. "Shall we spend the evening together?" "Yes!" she said as if she wanted to please him and a faint blush rose in her white cheeks. "Shall we say 8.30 at Café Pashing? Would that suit you?" She said that it suited her.

Only when the door closed behind her did he remember that he had promised to spend the evening with Emmy. Emmy was the wife of an estate owner outside Vienna but country life bored her and she spent the winter in her apartment in the city. They had been having an affair for some time. Emmy was elegant and intelligent. Her husband played an important role in Austria and they led a very high-profile social life. Benno had no desire to be part of that circle this evening and even less desire for Emmy's caresses. No, not Emmy this evening, and perhaps never again – he did not know why but he knew that now it was really over. He had tried to leave Emmy several times before but she had always laughed him out of it. He knew at this moment that his decision was made and his heart had already distanced itself from Emmy. He was happy to be spending the evening with Luise – she could have no idea how happy he was. He was as happy as a child on Christmas Eve. First he had to find an excuse to put Emmy off. He called; Emmy's voice was unexpectedly cool and she accepted his excuse without question. "Anyway" she said, "I have guests that you probably wouldn't like." He wondered what that could mean as he replaced the telephone receiver. Emmy was usually so clinging – too clinging he had sometimes thought.

He walked to the window again. The agitation of the last few days – no, the last few weeks was in his blood. Since the day four weeks ago when it was said that the Chancellor was in Berchtesgaden – that was the first sign of the dark clouds gathering on the horizon. Rumours flew around, people whispered amongst themselves in the cafés – but they said, after he had raged and roared, that the Chancellor had played fair, the newspapers were triumphant - Austria's independence was guaranteed. But there were doubts in the bravest of hearts. What was the Chancellor planning? Fear remained – the fear was Hitler, the demon fanatic, the insatiable.

The street seemed longer than usual. A light March wind brought the smell of fresh earth from Belvedere's gardens and the mountains. He breathed it in hungrily, the early spring smell, the breath of Vienna. Soon the violets in the Prater would bloom, the meadow flowers would follow and then the lilac trees on Heldenplatz would blossom; and in the Wienerwald it would be green. He walked along the old wall down to Schnarrenbergplatz. All over the ground lay shreds of paper, torn posters. Hail Schuschnigg! Hail Austria! But swastikas also lay all over the ground too, threatening signs, symbols of hate. Suddenly he was filled with a frightening tenseness. Was it just the echo of his footsteps that made him so nervous, or were the streets emptier and quieter than usual? He heard an hysterical cry Hail Schuschnigg, then the voice choked. On this early evening of 14 March Vienna was suddenly different. Vienna was ill. Suddenly from out of a window blared radio music which calmed him down a little. He suddenly remembered that Schuschnigg was about to give a speech in the Viennese Assembly. Perhaps everything will be alright after all, he thought, and turned and hurried home.

He ran up the stairs arriving out of breath and switched on the radio, thanking God as he heard Schuschnigg's familiar voice. But what was he hearing, the well-known voice was so different, so resigned, and what was he saying – it was unforgettable, ineradicable in his ears but his mind refused to make sense of it. His Austria, his beloved Austria had given up. There could be no disagreement – bloodshed must be avoided at all costs – and then almost with a sob Schuschnigg's voice saying "God save Austria." At these desolate words a sense of finality flowed through Benno and his whole body shook; he nearly collapsed. And now? God preserve – God protect. Then the Austrian national anthem, no longer sounding like a song of joy but a heartrending wail. A lament for Austria, drum rolls of pain.

Benno sat frozen as the hours passed. Then he sprang up – anything but be alone – be among people, talk to people. Suddenly he was out on the street again. There was Pienitzka, the porter, with a querulous expression on his face. He came from Bohemia and hated Hitler. "It is a shame, a shame Uncle Doctor," he growled as Benno passed him, but the cobbler at the corner standing arms akimbo in front of his shop stared at Benno and did not greet him. Where was the usual 'Honoured to see you Doctor' thought Benno with a bitter smile.

At Schnarrenbergplatz the Jewish paper seller held out a copy to him. "Vienna's last hour has struck" he said, "and the last hour for us Jews as well." Benno saw tears running down the old man's face where the memory of a thousand slaughters was etched. Benno thought of Luise. What did she know of the tragedy of the Jews? Would she even come to the coffee house, now when the world had so irrevocably changed? And if she did come, wasn't everything pointless and completely hopeless? Any idea of friendship would be impossible. Luise von Bruckner, the pious catholic officer's daughter and he, Benno Becker, the non-Aryan, the free thinker! Groups of people stood everywhere, with frightened faces whispering among themselves. Benno looked around. On the surface the city was unchanged, but the lights seemed paler and dimmer, the buildings greyer and ghostly. He stopped by the Opera house and stood for a while – he didn't know for how long, with thoughts and pictures running through his head. He had known for a long time that Vienna was ill, but there had always been a little hope left that things would improve. But now, in this last hour, Austria had died. Austria, his dear beloved old Austria that had given the world Mozart with his divine genius. Austria, along whose rivers the titan Beethoven with lowered head had struggled with the elemental force of melody within him; of Grillparzer; of Arthur Schnitzler and of Hofmannsthal. What did they all have to do with Hitler? Nothing – and now Austria, their Austria was dead. 'Heil Hitler, heil – heil' rang out coarsely from a side street.

Benno pulled himself together and went slowly towards Café Pashing, he walked slower and slower. He was convinced that she would not be there. Perhaps she had stayed at home to celebrate Hitler's victory. And if she did come, what was there to say? The abyss between them was too wide and too deep – there was no bridge.

The clock struck half past eight as he walked into the café. It was quiet. As the door closed the awful noise was shut out. The room was dimly lit and almost empty. The waiters stood around in groups and whispered amongst themselves. An old man bent over his newspaper and devoured it and a young couple with their eyes fixed on each other existed in their own world as if the terrible events of the day had not happened. Benno walked slowly through the room. He saw Luise, half hidden in a corner. She had come! Benno breathed out, it was the first happy moment in that terrible day, that 14 of March. He sat down beside her and reached for her hand. He saw that she was even paler than usual.

"Luise, I am so happy that you have come, but will you not regret it – later – when what must happen happens? You see, I am a Jew."

"I know," she said and looked him directly in the face. "I know." She was silent but her sad eyes were fixed on his face. Benno felt he was wrong to feel as he did and of course he wanted her to be happy, but her pale face and sad eyes meant so much more to him than if she had been cheerful. Nevertheless he felt he had to ask if she welcomed what had happened. After a pause, and haltingly, she said "Yes, of course, in a way – it had to happen sooner or later and you will see – lots of things will be better now". He answered sadly "I can understand why you think that way. How could you possibly not! But for me, and for thousands of others, everything is finished. Our Austria no longer exists. It would be better to die." He was surprised to see tears spring to her eyes. With a quivering voice she said quietly "It is terrible to hear you say such things Doctor. I - I have only experienced happiness with you, and your book – it is so wonderful – you are a poet – I felt that straight away and you know so much more than others, even about music which I love so much and when you talk about Vienna it is just so perfect. Of course I didn't tell you, but my aunt was beside herself when I said that I was working for a Jew. When I talk about how happy I am being with you…" Luise blushed scarlet as the words slipped out, "…my aunt gets really angry and says that you set out to ensnare me. My cousin Klaus wants me to marry him. He has been unemployed for ages but now he has found a good position although he never does anything properly and is very lazy. He gets even angrier about you than my aunt does and says he will pay you back for stealing me away from him. I know it is all nonsense and it is bad, but the truth is we have always been at loggerheads. They both say that the Jews cause trouble, that the Jews make money out of others and that the war is their fault and they let others fight for them. It is so difficult for me. Sometimes I don't know what to believe – especially now that I know you. But surely nothing will happen to you – they can't mean people like you."

"Do you really think that, Luise?" Benno's words sounded bitter. "I do mean it, really." she insisted. "You will see everything will get better in Austria."

"Better for Austria? No, no! a thousand times no." Then it all poured out of him; all the pain, the disappointment, the fear, the horror that had been locked inside him for so long. Not only since he had known Austria was threatened, but since the day that Germany had given Hitler their resounding acceptance. He wasn't only talking to the girl sitting beside him, but also to all the invisible enemies, to all those who couldn't, or wouldn't, see what was coming. He knew! He pitched his voice against the voices outside with their howling Heil Hitler. He spoke of

Austria, of how he loved it – had loved it since his childhood. He spoke of his mother, how good and kind she was. How she had brought her children up through great hardship; of his father who had fallen in the Great War when he, Benno, was just a small boy. Of how so many had thought that war would put everything right. He spoke of his uncle who had financed his studies; of the growing anti-Semitism in Vienna. Then he spoke of Judaism, of the Jews, God's chosen people. Chosen to suffer, eternally damned, always outsiders, never to be trusted; of the ever repeating cycle of being hunted. Then he painted a picture of the future: hate, violence, greed – never justice. Hitler, and with him another war, a war of terror more murderous than ever before. He asked her whether she believed that the people outside really knew what they had wished upon themselves. Benno spoke passionately, not caring that the waiters were listening. He saw only Luise's white face and her startled eyes. He was only concerned that she knew – that she understood – he didn't care about anyone else. While he was talking he had grasped her hand and was squeezing it without realising it, now he released the pressure and sat looking at her. Her eyes were filled with tears. "I did not know all that, I have never talked to people other than ordinary people - like those outside. I have been so stupid, I believed them all, my aunt, Klaus, the neighbours...... Everybody joined the 'movement'. The men got out their old uniforms and marched up and down the street. Klaus brought my aunt a swastika to wear so that nobody would think she was a Jew – but I wouldn't let her wear it because of you." Benno pressed her hand in thanks for her words. They sat together in silence for a long time. Benno was full of endless tenderness and thankfulness for the precious hours with Luise.

"But what will you do?" asked Luise. "If everything happens in Austria as you believe it will – what will you do?" And then, with a frightened passionate intensity "You must leave Vienna, you must not wait and get caught up in such things – you must be able to work – you must finish the book –

you must leave Austria." Luise had just put into words what Benno had known in his subconscious for some time. Yes, he had to leave Vienna, leave his beloved Austria, and leave this girl who looked at him with sad eyes. At that moment Benno knew that Luise had stolen his heart and that he loved her – loved her – loved her.

And now he had to gather all his strength, to overcome, to get over it, to forget. "I shall go, perhaps the day after tomorrow. I shall go to England, my younger brother is there. The English seem to know more than we do. He wrote several weeks ago saying that he had set things up so that in case of an emergency I would be able to get out." Every scrap of colour disappeared from Luise's face and her hand, which was still in his, began to shake. "But I can still come tomorrow?" she asked with a weak voice, "perhaps I can help with things – please, please say yes!"

They left the café together. Outside it was quieter than before but there were still groups of worried looking people standing on the pavement, and from the direction of the Opera house they could still hear calls of Heil Hitler. Benno took Luise's arm and said, "I shall see you to the tram, it has got late." As they got to Karlsplatz they heard the noise of motorbikes and then they saw the first German uniforms.

The few hours that Benno slept that night were filled with wild dreams. Huge black swastikas like grinning faces hung over his bed. Blood dripped from red flags. Wailing crowds of people pushed him along and behind them a creature with a large white beak was chasing him. When he awoke, everything was mixed up in his mind – had yesterday really happened? He ran to the window; sunshine and birdsong – then suddenly a child's voice shouted Heil Hitler! He switched on the radio, deafening military music blared into the room followed by the harsh voice of the Führer. He switched the radio off, dressed hurriedly and as he began to pack his elderly cleaning woman arrived, just as she had every day for many years. "The doctor is leaving us?" she asked, startled at the sight of the suitcase.

"Just for a few days, Mrs Lappert," said Benno hoping that his voice sounded indifferent. "I fear the Doctor is leaving for good." she said. "Whatever makes you think that, Mrs Lappert? I am really only going for a few days – at most I shall be back in a couple of weeks. Please tell anybody who asks you." "Of course, of course I shall do as you ask, but I know…." and Benno heard her sniff. "I know I shall never see the Doctor again." "But please Mrs Lappert…" She was crying, "It is so terrible that such a kind gentleman as you are dear Doctor must leave because of such happenings…." "But Mrs Lappert, I really do not know what you mean, and nothing will change for you." "No? How shall we simple folk fare when all the best people are leaving Vienna? Remember I have known you dear Doctor since you were a boy and I knew your dear father too. It is a real shame and a disgrace that even in Favoriten where we live there are rowdies on the streets. In our alley, Fleischmann's windows were all smashed, because he is a Jew, and Grünlein the jeweller was dragged out of his bed because he scrubbed away the swastika that had been painted on his door…..and he an old man! They have turned the head of my Mizzi's boy….yesterday Poldi came home shouting that they had thrown the Jews out of school and that they would get what was coming to them. Mizzi gave him a clap round the head of course, and he shouted that if she ever did it again he would denounce her to the authorities. We are all frightened out of our skins and it will not be long before everybody leaves the way Hitler is talking."

"For heaven's sake," said Benno quietly "be careful what you say near the open window. Don't get yourself into trouble. Take care and I thank you for all you have done for me." "Please dear Doctor, you must come back when it's all over," sobbed the old woman, "Come and ask for me, if I am still alive. Oh, it is such a shame!" The old woman closed the door behind her and Benno listened to her footsteps going slowly down the stairs. "Another bit of Austria that is gone forever," thought Benno sadly.

As he closed the large suitcase, Luise arrived. She was out of breath. "You are ready to go? Thank heavens! Did you hear – they marched over the border in the night. I am so afraid for you, I have heard such horrible, awful things. They have gone wild and there is a mob marching through Vienna – I would never have believed it. Are you sure you can get out? My aunt was angry when I said I was coming here today. I have to be back by lunchtime. It is so awful for me now, for I have no-one but you." "Yes, everything is organised – I just have to collect my visa. Come with me Luise, give me these last few hours; they will not be so sad if you are with me."

She looked at him with tear filled red eyes. "I don't know how I could have been so stupid, why did I never question anything? I have spent the whole night thinking about it and I am ashamed of myself. Early this morning I had an argument with my family. My aunt said that if I do not agree with her I must go and live somewhere else and when Karl came home he threatened me." "Luise, that must not happen – I don't want to make trouble for you. You belong with your people." Benno was trying to be fair to her and meant what he said, but at the same time he was filled with happiness, like the previous evening; one soul, this precious soul, was perhaps saved. "I want to spend as much time with you as possible," was all that Luise answered.

Out on the street everything was changing – motorbikes were filling the air with noise, trucks full of bales of red cloth were everywhere. Many people were wearing swastikas and bright armbands. On Schnarrenbergplatz tall masts were being put up and the Ring was full of marching crowds shouting Heil Hitler. In a tree sat a boy shouting with a hoarse voice. "He has hardly any voice left from shouting," said Luise. "It is quite frightening."

The old town was jammed with people – the pulse of Vienna was racing. Was it really still Vienna? Strange faces, strange vehicles, strange voices. Why was everyone staring up at the Stefanskirche? A huge red flag hung there and the black sign on it fluttered mockingly in the wind. Luise held on to Benno's arm and in a distressed whisper said "I would never have believed it." They turned into a quieter alley. When they reached the British Embassy they saw a long queue of people and joined it. Men and women stood there and Benno saw faces that he recognised and suddenly they all looked years older – in one night! When he finally got to the head of the queue and received his visa he asked Luise to stay with him a bit longer. He wanted just one more walk though Vienna, once more along the Ring. They walked along to Heldenplatz, there he took a last look at everything and let it imprint itself on his memory. By the fountain in the Rathaus park he had played as a child; as a school boy he had had his first rendezvous in the Volksgarten. In the winter everything had been illuminated, the front of the Rathaus had turned into a large present; the filigree decoration on the church tower sparkled. It all seemed like a dream. Could it really be that he would never see it again? – that he must go and never come back? Never walk with Luise again? In sorrowful silence they walked to Karlsplatz and he pressed her hand. "I shall come again tomorrow," said Luise. "Luise, that would be so nice, but you must not invite trouble for yourself at home."

"Oh, they are so stupid and so ignorant – I see it now. It is so awful for me; I just want one more day with you."

"Luise," he said and was suddenly animated and almost cheerful, "I should so like to take you out of the city, out of this trouble, it would be so nice, shall we – tomorrow?"

"Oh, how lovely," and "It warms my heart," came the answer immediately. They made plans to meet early the next morning at the tram station in Meidling.

Benno went to the Brown Stag where he was a regular guest. Loud laughter came from a table where four people were sitting. They were Germans and the table was littered with beer and wine bottles. Many of the regular guests were missing. An elderly doctor sat at his usual table but for once not alone. His son, who like Benno had just sat his doctoral viva, was there as well as a young girl, hardly more than a child. Her thin face had a pained expression and that of the young man was full of defiance. The old man spoke to them - at them - begging and pleading. Benno caught the odd sentence; "You must be sensible children," and "You are heading straight for trouble," and then the awful words "racial defilement." A shock ran through Benno at these words. He thought of his cousin Fritz in Germany who had also not wanted to leave his beloved girl - they were both now in Dachau. He thought again that he must leave and the sooner the better. He ate quickly, paid his bill to the waiter who was not as chatty as usual, and went home. Once there he tried to be organised; he burnt a lot of papers and then continued packing. Of course, he would have to say goodbye to Emmy and a few other friends. It would not do just to disappear without a word. He dialled Emmy's number and asked for her. The maid asked him to wait and then came back to the telephone to say that the lady of the house was out and that he should not bother calling again as she might be leaving town. Oh well, he thought, she is no longer anything to do with me. He called a few friends. They all sounded worried and unwilling to talk, but several hinted that they too would be leaving.

Yes, that was the other side of Vienna's bright laughing image: the victor's celebrations and the woes of the oppressed; Heil Hitler being shouted in the streets, deafening military music and whispers, secret flight and deadly terror.

The next morning Benno was awoken by a strange noise. At first a humming, getting nearer and louder every minute and finally becoming a deafening roar. What was it? Benno had never heard anything like it. Then he saw; planes, like huge black birds, came over the horizon, filling the skies. Now they were over Vienna, these German harbingers of death. The city almost shrank into itself under this threatening onslaught – "Bloodshed must be avoided at all cost," Schuschnigg had said; it no longer seemed possible thought Benno sadly. He knew he must leave; there was no future for him in Vienna – only danger and perhaps because of him danger for Luise too. But this last day, he thought defiantly, belonged to them. He wanted, just for one day, to forget; to enjoy his homeland just once more. He thought of Luise now as his homeland.

Benno went to the tram stop. There were lots of people on the street and flags fluttered from many of the houses. Why this flying of flags – was it in protest or in welcome? When the tram arrived, crowds of people descended as if they were going to a festival. The road out of the city was almost empty. Benno began to breathe freely again as the crowds and the flags were left behind. At the tram station in Meidling Luise was waiting.

They walked along arm in arm, shaking off the worry of the last few days. Here it was like another world and they were surrounded by pleasant and gentle peace; the little yellow cottages sat happily bathed in pale sunlight and children played in the small gardens. The tension that Benno had felt for the last few days began to ebb. He was happy listening to Luise's light step beside him and her arm through his brought him warmth and comfort.

They arrived unnoticed at the gates of the Hietzinger Cemetery and wandered in silence along the rows of grave stones. They stopped in from of a plain grey marble headstone. On the stone was engraved in large letters 'Dollfuss', and underneath 'His loyal people'. Here lay a piece of Austria. Here lay the first victim. Benno bent down distressed and picked a few ivy leaves and placed them on the stone. "In memory of our great Dollfuss," he said with a shaking voice. Luise took his hand and her eyes filled with tears. As they turned to go they saw that his widow was standing behind them. Dressed in worn old fashioned garments, her hands were folded and her lips murmured a prayer as she crossed herself. Benno thought to himself that it was good that Dollfuss was not completely forgotten, despite his sad end, and he hoped that he lived on in the hearts of thousands of Austrians and not only in the heart of his widow.

Benno and Luise left the city of the dead behind them and climbed up the hill. Spring was beginning to appear through the wintry vegetation. At the top, on flat ground, stood the little chapel surrounded by trees.

They sat together on the stone bank in front of the chapel. The ground fell away on all sides and the whole landscape was spread out before them stretching to the mountains in the distance. At the edge of the valley lay the Wienerwald and then the city encircled by a pale milky stripe – the Danube. Vienna – Vienna rang in Benno's head; city of emperors – city of the people! From grey stone the city had grown along the Danube – from where Benno and Luise sat they could see the buildings around the cathedral of St. Stefan, the unchangeable heart of Vienna. Over the centuries the city had grown – stretching almost to the hill with the little chapel. The city, its churches and cloisters; the baroque grandeur of the Karlskirche – its building faithfully recorded by the Capuchin chroniclers – where the dying Habsburgs were granted eternal rest. The gem – Maria of Sistade – built on the banks of the Danube that thundered over the rocks but never threatened the church. The thousands of Viennese people born in the houses of the city, and the thousands that slumbered in the cemeteries. The beautiful city of Vienna given to its people and their children; how could it now be given to the tyrant; how could the people be so thoughtless and careless; how could they not see that there would be no peace in war; that Vienna would be turned into a German war machine? "You will come back!" Benno heard Luise's gentle voice beside him. "Do you really believe that?" he said sadly and doubtfully. "And if I do what will there be here for me?" He was thinking of her as he spoke; the beautiful creature who had become so precious to him in these few short days. She was one of the 'others', but he wished and hoped that she could be his.

They wandered back down the hill and went to a small restaurant on the edge of the city. "You have chosen the right place" said their pretty and friendly hostess. "Here everything is still as it should be, but some people out there have lost their minds over Hitler, and what are they doing to the poor Jews? Vienna is no longer the city with the golden heart!"

Smilingly Benno ordered Wienerschnitzel and Kaiserschmarren for their last meal together and an especially good bottle of wine, an Empoldskirchen '19. He was happy as they sat down at the little table and the Empoldskirchen was sublime. They toasted each other and Luise's cheeks were flushed a pale pink, her faun-brown eyes were shining and her beautiful lips were moist. "How beautiful she is," thought Benno who could not stop looking at her. "How beautiful she is – but it is all pointless. She will marry an SS man and be happy. I must leave this evening and tomorrow I shall be over the border – it is all pointless." Abruptly he stood up. "We must go!" he said suddenly. As they walked towards the bridge he wondered how to say goodbye. It is so awful he thought, I must shake her hand and wish her well for I shall never see her again. Luise was thinking the same sad things, "I should like to come home with you," she said. Their hands remained locked together until they reached the house. When they reached his apartment Luise threw herself into an armchair, buried her face in her hands and began to cry softly. Benno stood before her and stroked her hair with shaking hands. "Luise – dearest girl, I didn't want you to be upset. You belong to the others; you have to do as they say. Perhaps everything will work out and you will be safe and happy." "Don't say such things, please, please. I don't belong with them anymore. They are all so stupid and so bad. Oh, why didn't you come into my life earlier, or perhaps why did you come at all?"

First Benno kissed her blonde hair and her hands. Then he pulled her to him. He was amazed at her willingness to fall into his arms. Passion coursed through his veins. No, no! he almost cried aloud, this must not happen. Tomorrow I shall be far away from her – I shall never see her again – I must not ruin her life. Perhaps she will understand when I am gone - if she loves me she will understand – I must not spoil her chance of a life without me – a future among her own people. I would hate myself forever.

"Luise, dear beloved Luise – I beg you – you must go. I beg you – if you love me, go!" "Yes, yes – I am going," she whispered through bloodless lips. He held her to him once more, covered her face with kisses and said again, "Go…" She went to the door and then turned and said, "I shall always love you. I shall never forget you." The door closed and he was alone.

Benno threw himself across his bed and cried. He cried more bitterly than he had ever done. It was as if a volcano had erupted; as if all the endless pain and hurt long buried within him had broken out with elemental force. His body was racked with sobs as he felt his whole world crumbling around him. He had lost everything – everything; his homeland which was his air and light and Luise – his Luise. Only strangers and loneliness awaited him now. The hours until his train left seemed endless. He sat, with his head in his hands. He kept reaching for the telephone to call Luise, just to hold her close once more, just to hear her voice …… He did not call.

At last it was time. He took the small suitcase; the rest of his luggage was to be sent on. Pienitzka pulled a long face when he saw Benno's suitcase. "It's the right thing Uncle Doctor. I would go too if I could. Things will only get worse here." Benno shook his hand and then climbed into the taxi. On the way to the station he took his leave of Vienna, but again it no longer seemed to be the Vienna he knew – the shouts of Heil Hitler, the noise of the motor cycles, the marching soldiers, the bright lights and the flares in the darkness. The West Station was crowded with taxis and luggage and the train hall packed with people. Many whispered amongst themselves and looked around afraid at the uniformed men, mostly young, bedecked with armbands and swastikas – the rough hard faces of the victors. The train was overcrowded, every place was taken. Oh well, thought Benno, I shall have to stand all the way; but what does it matter, I shouldn't be able to sleep anyway. He looked at the people in the train. Every single face told the story of its own personal tragedy – so many lives had been changed and destroyed in the last few days. There was an old mother, holding onto the hand of her son through the window; and there a man with tears pouring down his face not wanting to let go of his child while its mother stood crying silently; a young girl threw herself into the arms of her lover probably for the last time. Faces frozen in stone and hands wrung endlessly in desolation. Benno blessed the fact that his mother had not lived long enough to see that day. Then he felt again the pain of the loss of his beloved Luise and suddenly he saw her pale form fighting her way through the crowds of people. He leapt out of the carriage. "Luise, beloved girl – it is so wonderful that you have come – so wonderful. But the train is about to leave – I don't want to leave you. Oh why have you come? – I cannot leave you again!"

"They threw me out of the house – because I told them the truth – that they are wrong and that – that I love you!" she said through her tears. His heart leapt, "Come with me Luise. Luise – forever – stay with me forever. Have you a passport? Yes, you have it. We can wait in Switzerland for your visa. My brother in London will help us, I am sure of it. Everything will be alright if you love me." Benno helped Luise into the train which slowly began to move. Gradually they left the lighted station, and Vienna and the nightmare of the last few days sank into the darkness behind them. In his arms Benno held the girl who had now become his homeland, and together they headed towards the unknown.

Translated by Antonia Brotchie

Appendix II: Lisi's Diary

9 Bardwell Road, Oxford

Friday 1 Sept. 1939

Oxford. I feel so relieved, almost happy to be here. Despite all the tension, despite the threat of war! At the end Berlin was a nightmare. I felt so terribly abandoned. I was frightened of staying. I had no people, no-one to talk to. Perhaps I just missed a little bit of comfort, warmth, culture outwardly and inwardly. I was afraid of getting ill, without help, with no-one to talk to. I was afraid of lonely hours, dark nights, even of myself, being 'left to myself'. How good it is to be here. In a pretty, well-kept Oxford home, with gentle disciplined people, I am happy with my friendly room, where I can have all my things. A room with hot water, with a garden and a well-kept table. And the view from the window that looks onto a dear little garden filled with velvety green grass and many colourful flowers.

Apart from the owners of the house, there is a blind gentleman with his wife. He unsettled me, like every blind person, but not painfully. He has wonderfully elegant hands; he speaks more clearly and calmly than most other people. But of course he has his wife with him, gentle and kind, reading nothing from his blind eyes but every thought from his high forehead. She must have been an incredibly beautiful creature when she was young; and then such an intelligent elegant husband. Now they are both old and he is blind. ------- I hope the postman brings me news tomorrow. Hugo is still stuck alone out in Hampshire. Nature and that 'special girl' keep him there. As long as he is happy, I must let him do as he wants. I have read 'Sodom's Ende' again. He, Hugo, is splendid, with all his weaknesses! There is so much in him. He is dignified and noble, and even if sometimes he fails in daily life, <u>he is really splendid</u>. Henry-- Henry is dear, good and clever.

Saturday 2 Sept.

No letters came. The old couple have gone to Cornwall. The blind gentleman must hear as little as possible about the war – if it does break out – no-one can really believe that it will. To be blind and then to know that the seeing are fighting must be terrible. I call Henry. He is coming straight away. Once again my world is good and happy. Unbelievable! We must all avoid showing any light tonight. ------ Henry came much later than I expected. It got dark, black dark outside. I made my way through the half-dark house to the street. I couldn't even see the pebbles on the gravel path through the garden. I listened to every distant footfall, listened for every car, to every voice that came from out of the dark. It started to rain gently. Hours later the beloved voice saying 'Thank you so much'. A woman had led him here, a complete stranger. They are all so kind, so unquestioningly helpful.

Sunday 3 Sept.

It was in church. A note was passed to the priest whilst he spoke. He covered his face with both hands – We are at war. My heart started beating fast and I felt a little dizzy, but I was not as desperately sad as perhaps I should have been – I don't know. There seemed to be a spark of happiness, God will fight against the Devil – the good against the bad. And I stood next to Henry, kneeled next to Henry - how could I be really sad? He is leaving early for London, while it is still dark.

Monday 4 Sept.

Dead in Poland, women and children. A ship has been torpedoed – many wounded. Here there is great calm and discipline. On the street I notice that so many couples are holding hands, have their arms around each other. Many smile – but perhaps I only notice because I make a conscious effort to notice everything.

Tuesday 5 Sept.

Wonderful autumn days. Everything dressed in a dense glowing green, and roses everywhere. Roses and colourful autumn flowers. The skies are a pale blue with little white lambswool clouds. Aeroplanes – perhaps bombers? I cannot get it into my head! – How unbelievably beautiful must the sea be, blue like the sky, little white-tipped waves ----- and then a ship torpedoed on this beautiful sea, a ship sunk and all the corpses.

Wednesday 6 Sept.

Early in the morning the first air raid. In the dark coal cellar, a few people and Tiny, the dog. Everyone, even the dog, stays calm. I too, of course, it would be shameful not to. To be honest though, so far I have not felt afraid.

Thursday 7 Sept.

I can only marvel. In actual fact I <u>ought</u> to be unhappy. So many troops already in Poland, they apparently just walked in – so many dead and wounded along the lines of fighting. People in misery and danger – Mama, Emmy, Max. It is all so frightful, mankind seems to have lost its soul. Is it the brilliant heavens, the light, the green, the flowers, the mellow city, the calm, kind people here that make me feel almost happy? Or is it a deep, almost subconscious joy that mankind has woken up and is fighting against the evil? H so often called me the 'world's conscience'. Perhaps I am spared the worst worry because I no longer feel as alone as I often used to. But for the others, those in fear, I must be still and pray. For me, praying is looking for the deepest and best in us all.

Friday 8 Sept.

I go for walks, like all the others, with my gas mask, tied to a piece of pink lingerie ribbon (I had nothing else) hanging around my neck and over my shoulder. I go like all the others down to one or other shelter. Outside a harvest sky and hazy sunshine.

Wednesday 13 Sept.

Hugo has gone. It was so good, better than for a long time – despite his studied nonchalance. So tall, so lean with his sometimes wise and sometimes childlike head. He is such a specially pure, noble and rounded person, but with a few family weaknesses – as the sun has sunspots. I criticise him and then he does the same to me. I love him so much and must help him, but my dumb, touchy young boy does not understand that. But I believe that he does love me too, in his way. He handles the outbreak of war better than I imagined. He is living is a cottage, just the sort of place he loves, with fields all around and has his beloved with him.

Ada has written from Switzerland. Her tragedy gets bigger all the time. Mother and the man whom she adores, are still in Vienna, unreachable, and her Thea is in Canada, almost on another planet. What a fate, threatening and uncertain – like a storm!

(A page is missing here)

From where comes such certainty? That Hitler's end is nearing, that those people who supported him will turn away from him, that the others will win, that those who disappoint me, near and far, will wake up and realise what is right and good, and that my children ......

16 Sept.

In Memoriam. My Lilli, when your husband wrote to me of your death, it was not at first so difficult to accept. We hadn't seen each other for a long time, and I said to myself: she did not have much to live for. But one's heart is wilful. Every day my heart reminds me on waking that you, my old Lilli are no longer alive, and as well as the pain there is a great wound. How is it possible that you are no more? You were always larger than life. Even when you were ill, when you said that you had had more than enough, you were still livelier than all the others. You were the eternal flame, shining bright, demanding, encouraging and glowing. Sometimes you were beset by worries, but still you were aflame. And this eternal flame gave you a grandiose light in everything you did and thought far out into the future....no, if you could have seen into the future you would have seen that there was a war coming – this war with Hitler – whom you so wished for – perhaps then you would not have been so happy. You once wrote to me saying that you would fight if Germany placed even one foot on Dutch land. Perhaps you would still say the same. Perhaps I am just a little angry with you because you deserted me with such ease. God knows how you could leave me so alone! Perhaps you realised that you couldn't help me. But you were you to the end! Alien soul! Sister heart! Oh Lilli. I do not want to idealise you, now that you are dead. Clever, cool schemer that you were! I called you the 'snake from the Nile' – and you laughed! You were like the emerald that you wore, poisonous green with golden lights, but one saw the gold so seldom – but you were so precious. You outshone all the other precious gems....that such a small hand could wear such an emerald ring –

That someone that one loves can cause such hurt......

18 Sept.

Such acknowledgement and warmth amongst strangers...... one's nearest and dearest are too much. All of mine are ungrateful, bigoted and completely without self-critique. As if they had a wall around them so that nothing gets to them. I don't believe in horoscopes and such things, but whoever said the prophetic words....the family are the least grateful and take the least notice. Must one really be dead before one can be appreciated?

Sadly the Germans are enjoying great successes. Poland is overrun, so many people are dead, mostly civilians. Can such awful things be reversed?

I had several good hours with Miss H.C. We talked about TJ. My heart is all stirred up. I loved him so much. Even today I do not know how or why it came about. He was so much greater than all the others. It was definitely not ordinary.

19 Sept.

Outside my window a pale blue evening sky with touches of gold. Pale green tree tops stretch up to it. Quiet. – and somewhere outside, the chattering, hammering of machine guns and women and children meeting a frightful death.

20 Sept.

Not good news from the front lines. Is there still anyone alive in Poland? All the other 'fronts' are dangerous too. So many lies and such pain, terrible happenings and meanness. But here one sits in the park and chats – inside and outside the strangest feeling of peace. By day the green of the trees and silvery flowers – I am afraid my eyes deceive me with this silvery shine, but I see it anyway – and by night, everything darkened……..only not the moon. It hangs huge and clear in the shimmering tent of the heavens and is radiant. Beside it, myriads of stars – God doesn't join in the blackout.

22 Sept.

'Revolution' in Czechoslovakia! Strikers arrested! It is frightening. Hopefully it will not get unpleasant for all those there. Mothers and children – separated – as if in another world! They are so alone, the good ones – the innocents!

Sunday 23 Sept.

Henry is here. I am so happy to be with him. It is strange, in some ways I get on better with him and then in others better with Hugo. He cannot understand why Lilli's death upsets me so. It would be better to be less affected. Neither of them really understands why I wrote to Ernst. Some people have no-one close to them, don't understand the need to be there for someone etc. But I can only give everything, like Hedi, sadly also like Ernst K. (I still feel sorry for him!) as well as for Arthur B….there is still a little bit of love or hope there. I am afraid though that with Ernst and Irma the difference of type is too great, they have neither of them become sensible.

26 Sept.

Two sleeping children, brothers (refugees I think, evacuated from London). Sunday morning in Oxford, a bomb, left by a stranger…..heaven knows who. One child was badly wounded and died yesterday in hospital. Why? One could think about it forever and come to no conclusion. In Poland, the people have been fighting back. As the invading Germans saw what was going on they shot everybody they could see. Those left will starve they say. It is better not to think about it.
But now, something quite different: I have to finally admit it to myself and to the world….I do not like dogs and other

animals. I know for most people that is shocking. I do not do them any harm, but like them?? No. Dogs are not discerning, they love their masters even if they are liars and murderers. What is their love and loyalty really worth? I know some people put a lot of store by the loyalty of dogs, but really they are so unsavoury. Who would disagree with me? People offer their hand when they have touched the muzzle of a dog, which has probably just licked itself and its dirty feet. They walk through rubbish and I find it sickening.

27 Sept.

Mein Sisichen, At this moment your letter arrived! How wild is my heart! I suffer terribly. I want to go back, and I have the feeling that I have not been able to grasp happiness and that it is the last opportunity to lead a life of my own. Even the awful yearning for Mother and Max pales into insignificance beside it. My soul is ill. Yesterday another telegram from the children saying that I must come......would it help anyone? The ship on October 14 will not work .... should I go so head over heels? They send money! I should be happy to have such children. I am, of course, but cannot be happy about it. Sisi, what should I do. I am going to Holland in a few days. Please write to me there, or here, or both! Please! Max writes so sadly and begs me for news of you. Heinz must not. Please! Although I do understand! Kisses from both. Sisi, I will not be able to stand it. He is just as I love him! Sisi, why did I leave! Help me! I send you love, your ....Poor soul, you couldn't understand me then, but now you know that the last love, the love of the mature woman is the greatest, the fiercest and the most painful!

A man, sitting next to me on a park bench, reads his book and every now and then checks the meaning of a word in a glossary. I ask him: 'Is it a language you are learning?' 'No, I am not learning English, not everybody here is German, I am English, born English, for ever and ever!'

I meet the man from yesterday, again sitting on a bench and say to him: 'I am not German, I am born Czech, maybe my son will fight with you against Germany'. He says: 'Pardon me, I did not know it, but the Germans will kill my only son. And I hate the refugees, I am Quaker, I hate the refugees, they take our jobs'. When I meet him again I shall say: 'You are a hater, not a Quaker'. No, I shall not say anything. As the man spoke he went greeny-yellow in the face and his eyes blitzed like a madman.

1 October.

So Poland does not exist anymore. So much death, blood, sorrow and all for nothing. Or perhaps for something? For the idea of justice and freedom? Stalin and Hitler have joined forces, and fight against the others. So much dirt, lies and meanness on both their parts. But one can fight against them. Lillichen, you didn't live to see it, I am sad about that!

Hugo teaching. In a beautiful quiet place that is called Christchurch. Near the house, many green trees outside his window, but he is separated from the one he loves. I have wished him well.

2 October

A letter from Gerda, she has not given up as we thought. My clever Margit was mistaken. She is staying strong. She writes that she is seeing to the things I asked.

Wonderful autumn days. There are still pink roses between the green leaves and still water lilies on the pond, and still birdsong in the treetops. But many planes in the sky, day and night, an unpleasant droning noise, but still, praise God, not enemy ones.

2 Park Town, Oxford

10 October

Nothing written for a whole week. A new home. But again almost only good things. But for the ever increasing greyness, I could perhaps be happy. Despite the war, it is a disgrace, but it is so. There are speculations that Hitler wants peace, he is no longer the almighty and no longer certain of succeeding, fortune is no longer on his side. – Ada is in Amsterdam. She is not amusing herself very much. Having left the children in Vienna, she is being very good and quiet and cannot wait to get back to the children. Hedi tried to persuade me to go, saying I am soul sick. It is outrageous and not to be excused. She is either so dumb or so ill, and when a person shows a really nasty side of their character, I become indifferent to them and have no more sympathy for them ..... also 'he' doesn't appear to get things right always .... the unwilling honeymoon in Switzerland when work and children are in London. It was not good, to put it mildly.

14 October

Sister E,
Thank you for the card and the paper cuttings. From M I have sadly no further news, despite my many attempts, but I am happy not to have to worry and that Sisi and R are still alive. According to the latest news from Ada who is in Amsterdam, Max should be in Budapest already. – Hugo has been working as a teacher for some time now in Christchurch, but it is not certain that his work permit will be renewed. However, as Hugo teaches Latin, French and History as well as Music for a very small wage, the headmaster thinks that all will be well. Henry is doing his best to join the English Army in France, but must accept that he will not be paid. Things continue to go well

for me. Life here in Oxford is less expensive and more pleasant than in London and I have security (without the worry of being knifed in the back!). I do not want to mention your reply to my last letter. I think that had you taken more time and more thought over it you would have written differently. Simply the question as to whether 'my financial situation is really so dire' must be answered straight away. It is naturally not the case, as 80% of all refugees live from small pensions or work as domestic servants. My situation is, of course, not as good as yours, as I am not as fit and able as Irma, and see a time in the future when I shall be quite blind, but apart from that I am enjoying the quiet life here. I manage without any help, not that I would accept any anyway. I am no longer living with Miss M.C., as I was occupying her sister's room and the latter has now come from London to live here. I wish you both everything good and remain, with best wishes …..

Hedi bombards me with letters that she must have been mad, and that she will never forgive herself for having insulted those people who were nearest to her. I am sorry for her, but I am not a machine.

16 October

It is autumn. Rain, cold and damp fog; yellow leaves make the paths slippery. The owl calls in the evenings and even more in the mornings. A hateful and baleful sound! Many people say that Oxford is no less than safe. Masses of soldiers, so many beautiful young men amongst these beautiful old buildings – it should be tempting for the Führer! But this is all insignificant when I think of Henry crossing the Channel with the English Army. I hope my nerves will be strong enough to cope!! I am taking English lessons from an old cripple. I was shocked when I first saw him, a thin little man with crooked legs in a wheelchair, but the grey hair and the high forehead, the merciful expression and eyes sparkling with peace and happiness. Some people have a special strength ..... one must warm to them.

Beginning of November.

Cold and stormy, but one should perhaps not always wish for windless sunshine. Hitler says that if he could have 10 days of good weather, he could defeat England – we must welcome rain and storms. I keep myself together mostly but often it all seems very unreal. I don't go around Oxford very much as I feel very alone despite all the friends and acquaintances I have. My thoughts and feelings are always with the children, and they are both well. That is where my strength and calm comes from. Also my love for them is so strong that it often surprises me. One has three lives to live and suffer, but sometimes there comes from such a love huge happiness. Henry has good prospects for the future, everyone loves him. But how, in a war, like this one, can one build upon anything? The old man is pessimistic, and that startles me, as the pessimists in this world are usually right. Well, not always. Ada and H(arry) L.T. have found and love each other, and want to live their lives together. Just a few weeks ago she wrote that she was 'sick from love and longing' for him, he is the 'only one'. He wrote that he would follow Lilli, would always love her – and today? But it is right and good that he can be as he is. The pain of a broken heart makes one afraid of accepting love, but it grows as a seed.

3 November

It is four years today since Margit died. What has happened in these four years to me, to those around me, what has happened to the Earth – it is all so daunting that the human brain can hardly encompass it. One is dashed to the deepest depths and thrown to the highest heights – the greatest fall, the most awful suffering – the clearest days and the most gruesome nights of feeling – and in a land, in a house that once would have seemed for me the most alien. Harry despaired, he was berated, suspected, ignored and insulted. God, God, everything now is compensation! – a secure position with great prospects (cross fingers). That the once so simple acquaintance is married to a strange woman…he who trembled when Margit looked sideways at him…is now happy with another.

Lilli, the liveliest, Lilli, the soul nearest to my own, the glowing flame is out, the hand with the emerald is now dust like Margit's. Three weeks ago he wanted to commit suicide, he was finished with life…and today he writes the most wonderful love letters to Ada, who a few weeks ago had to leave her Viennese friend and is now on a lonely sea journey just longing for Harry who sits in Amsterdam and waits. – And then war!!

4 November

It is always the same with me. At first the ability to be really, really happy, but then the shadow of my melancholy sinks over every happy thing. I was honestly happy about Ada, – but now what worries me is why was I not equally lucky with my choice? Am I less deserving? Have I loved less? Suffered less? Olga Schnitzler once said: 'God lets his beloved ones suffer' – I would have been damaged thanks to that man if I had lived with him – but this grey nothing that came instead, this complete destruction of my soul – that was not and is not good and kind of you, dear God. And I have been given nothing to replace this complete destruction of my self-worth.

Henry is coming today – the clever, the noble, the admired, the disciplined one. Hugo worries me, his great intellect does not allow him always to stay above things, his clarity often fails and his heart is not always warm enough. He has much from his mother, but my incandescence for right is stronger. He is not the 'world's conscience' as Ernst once called me.

9 November

There are shadows in my feeling and thinking. The gaiety of the old Oxford is no longer there. Why? Is it psychological, is it physical? I still cannot fathom it. Is it the realisation of my own loneliness that spoils the happiness of Ada's luck in love? The realisation that life has not given me what it owes me, what I most long for – to be completely happy with someone else. Everything has gone wrong. That Fritz became ill, that was the first disappointment; then Ernst, who never really made me happy, more often unhappy; then Max, that good-natured but so charactery strange man; then Pfeiffer, who I thought was 'the one' and whom I loved more than all the others, and who treated me so abominably – completely obliterated me. Perhaps my sadness is the result of this disappointing love life. Perhaps the subconscious fear that bad can win, for Hitler is the devil and will not give up so quickly. Perhaps he will destroy himself. Ada's lover worries that she will not find her way back to him in Holland.

10 November

A bomb blast in Munich. Hitler, Hess, Goebbels, Streiker had all left the building 10 minutes earlier. The Pope!!!, Queen Wilhelmina and Mussolini congratulate Hitler on his escape.

13 November

Sometimes such a feeling of loneliness. More or less everyone strangers. What do they know of me and my life? And what could and might I tell them?!

The people in the house: perhaps the nicest Miss Lovegay. A little grey spinster, always suffering, always frightened of something or other. Devastated by rumours of the mistreatment of the Jews, she still manages to be friendly and benevolent to everyone, including me. Mrs King – outwardly accepting of foreigners, but I feel an inner resistance towards us. Miss Travers – kind, always with a book in her hand, uninteresting but good-natured. Miss Morley – stern, not at all nice, often catty, has fits of rage against refugees. Then Zummerkircher – who barks questions at people, bigoted and bad-natured. Enough to spoil any good mood. Mrs Treves – the lady, dignified and well-dressed. If I were English, we should certainly be friends, she has such a huge vocabulary – she is very talkative, very humane 'is it not with a full heart – not just show?' Dr. Rosen – a very German type – outwardly no Semitic gene – but perhaps – a critical brain, a bit Prussian, a bit worldly, a bit Jewish. A Viennese, Miss Schwarz – a realist, very prudent, excessive, aggravating, but humble and nice. A face that hides disappointment, full of sorrow and struggle, but dogged struggle. A high thin voice.

Lots of letters today, but nothing to help old wounds heal. Recognition, perhaps even loving thoughts? Nothing of the kind, only terrible setbacks.

21 November

Nervous, agitated and often very sad, but no more reason than in summer and autumn. Subconscious, I try to call everything to mind. Max? Yes, worry sits on me, however much I try to avoid it. Henry? The thought that he could go away and I would not know whether my beloved son is well, not in danger. And that so many people are suffering? That really distresses me. I try and keep it all together, I fight against it, but it makes me so frightened. This depression is the worst thing that has ever happened to me, and I have suffered a lot. I shall use everything good that is in me to defend myself. I regard myself as a good person, a moral person. A good conscience is good medicine. I hope that Max can feel the same.

26 November

I cannot deny it any longer. The good days in Oxford are over. The feeling of being happy has got lost, even worse, I cannot even imagine it anymore. Why? I pretend to myself that if I knew the reason I could do something about it. But I do not know the reason. Everything and nothing, it could be many things. Subconsciously in any case, not clear enough to bring to mind. Physical? Cause or effect? The weather? Storms and rain, and then clear heavens. None of it touches me. Much more the mines, the seas are strewn with corpses. The devil Hitler is still very powerful. Perhaps it is the loneliness; after all I am alone here. Only strangers around me. Those of my youth – none left. Lilli is dead. My mother – shall I see her again? Max – worry plagues me, that is the worst thing at the moment. I will fight against it; I must fight against it – because of the children.

29 November

A letter from Henry - written in English: "I admit that things are beginning to be more serious. But there is no reason to be disappointed or worried. Nobody could expect that the whole war is going to be nothing but a joke. I never believed that it will not be a hard struggle and that we shall not have to go through a lot of difficulties. They will find or they even have found means to fight the mines. I know it will mean that hundreds if not thousands of brave fishermen, who are volunteering for minesweeping, will sacrifice their lives, probably without a complaint. Is that quite the right moment to tell me to think things over and to be careful? You are quite wrong if you think that I only see the bright side of joining the Army, and do not realise its immenseness. I do not imagine for a moment that it is going to be all fun. It means hard work, lack of any comfort, discipline etc. I do not believe that it really means much more danger. In this war we are all in danger, a baby in its cradle or an old woman in her bed may be killed by a bomb, and a soldier in the front line may go through it all unharmed. I think it is all destiny, and if it has to come then I prefer it as a soldier in doing my duty instead of having remained at home. It is all very nice to say that I may be able to do more in a leading capacity than as an ordinary soldier. Perhaps I would be better as a cabinet minister or as some sort of diplomat, but I am afraid they won't offer me such a position, so I must serve in that way which is open to me."

This letter was from Henry. I see him when he was born, as a little bundle when he lay beside me; I see him taking cherries from my hand and giving them to others rather than eating them himself; I hear the teacher in Innsbruck saying that one day he will be a noble man – he was seven years old; I see him coming back from Leipzig, standing before me as Doctor, after the shortest study time, not having told anyone that he was taking the exams; I see him in countless photographs, always good and wise and always self-controlled. I stand in awe before my son. I love the other one no less – perhaps he has a difficult life – as I do. He is different from Henry, but also pure gold and precious.

4 December

This intangible, indefinable melancholy continues. If I had not already suffered such frightful depression I should not be so frightened now. I cannot fight against it in the same way. I am far more modest now, quite meek and I feel as if I have aged a hundred years. These were the years that I so loved, and so hoped to be loved in return – now I am an old woman with white hair. The world looks terrible. Ever darker clouds hang over the earth, lightning alarms us and storms lurk in the shadows. Will the sun ever shine again? Will the dark clouds ever go? Will the children ever be happy?

11 December

Everything that happens today, even more, everything that might happen, can only be borne in a sort of trance. One must look death in the eye. Not only as a soldier. Those who really admit what is happening, those who stand fully in life, can hardly bear it. It is too much for the mind to encompass and not give up. I worry about Max. I would give so much to know that he is safe and well……at least safe from the evil. Everything else appears easy in comparison. Why do I have to suffer for him as well? Wasn't worrying about him for years already enough? Worry greater than happiness?! Once he was kind and helpful, and because of that I feel permanently at fault. He was with me when I was ill, and therefore I need to be there for him if he is in danger. It is awful that I cannot be there for him – it is the worst thing.

14 December

Mr Cutcliff said that if there can be God there can also be the devil, and all the troubles of the world are the eternal battle between them. If so, it was the devil's work that caused the father and his two children to drown, and the woman, the mother to live on alone. Karl Gresitz and his two children went down with the 'Simon Bolivar'. The ship was torpedoed. They were on their way to Suse in Montevideo. So many brave people. The children still certainly innocent, sinless. Karl sent my mother flowers the last time he was in Vienna. He has my eternal thanks for that. Walther Fischer is dead. He was my age, a childhood friend and classmate. When will it be my turn?

Between Christmas and New Year

My worst fear has been realised. Max did not get away. I shall copy out the letter telling me about it, but not today. I must keep such things away from me, I must stay well, or the feeling of guilt will take over completely. I am afraid of myself, afraid of my scrupulous conscience. I see no way out for Max. I should like to be able to redo many things. One speaks often of compensation. He was almost in safety, happy and content, but not I. I find no comfort in these thoughts. And my eyes are a problem.

31 December 1939

The year draws to an end. What has it brought us? What has it taken from us? The children are here with me. They are healthy and so far happy. That is the most important thing. War, the threat of war. It couldn't go on like that. I was almost happy when war was declared. – What happened to Max was bad luck. For him and for me. How will things end for him? For me, I had expected to be with him when things came to an end. Shall I spend the rest of my life alone now? Perhaps ill, old and blind? How will it be, the end of sight? The thought is almost unbearable, how will the actuality be?

The year did bring something – the absolute, the certain, the permanent 'no' for my love. The sorrow that I have already suffered on behalf of this man could not increase anymore – but now I am finally old and nearing the end through him and because of Lilli.

16 January 1940

Does not the word 'happy' appear on the first page of this book? How was that now? I can no longer call those feelings to mind however hard I try. Was the world so different? Did I see it with other eyes? Today there is danger and suffering everywhere. Mankind is distressed wherever one looks. War, earthquakes, cold, perfidy, all vices and devilry triumphing. One becomes blunt trying to come to terms with it all. I try not to see, not to hear many things. I try not to think about Max…it would make things unbearable. I try to comfort myself with the thought that everybody everywhere is in danger. My inner voice says 'freedom', but it isn't. Shall I see mother and sister again? I should be so happy to be with Emmy. I feel we are closer than ever now. And mother is so old!

24 January

I do not understand it. This sadness comes and goes and I cannot control it. Is it the body or the soul that subconsciously makes me feel sad? There are enough reasons to be sad, but despite all these I used not to feel this way. I saw everything differently, felt differently. I thought I was safe forever from melancholy, from despair. Now I am again afraid that my sorrow is like that of those frightful months when it broke me down. Why cannot I forget this awful happening and get over it? But all my loved ones have become so distant that I don't understand them anymore. Even Ernst is distant and strange and indifferent to me. Why does this plague and pain me so? Why does he leave me so unhappy, without hope, with no relief…..how is it possible? Perhaps because I didn't really love him the way I loved the others – perhaps I loved him too much, with my whole being, because I trusted him, I believed that I had finally found my soul mate who felt the same for me. He was so awful to me, so murderous, - why can I not hate him, reject him? It is because I have tied myself up in guilt and self-accusations. I thought of myself and not of him when he was suffering. He was supposed to love me, to respect me, to take care of me. Knowing this causes me endless sorrow. That is why no-one can save me or help me. It is all my fault. I no longer like myself. This is the worst feeling that a human being can have.

23 February

After the cold, the snow and the winter storms, there is a first idea of spring. Air, light, earth – promising. I see it and feel it, but I am not quite present, because I no longer have a future. I should like to live to see one more thing: Hitler defeated, destroyed, so that the children have a better world to live in. My children and all those who yearn for something better. It will take a long time, so far nations and people are too weak-minded and lazy hearted. Only the bad are powerful and willing to fight. I hear that Max is well and not unhappy. How often did he say that he wouldn't want to be me! Perhaps this time I have suffered more than he!

Sunday 25 February

Lilli – I have to write to you today, I need to talk to you as we used to. Death has not taken you far from me. Sometimes you feel even closer than the others, of whom many are on the other side of the world …… although no-one is so eternally far away as you are, my dead but ever living Lilli. So much about you was not good or right, how often this or that irritated me, but despite all that Dear Lilli, you were always so wonderfully close to me, chasing away the loneliness, spreading light everywhere, related through choice. In one thing I did you wrong; I believed that you were insincere, that your good words meant nothing. Now when I am really sad and tired, I sit and write to you asking for them, I who rejected them. Now that you can no longer hear the birdsong, you can no longer see the skies, which today are grey in my window; do you know how much I think of you with love and longing?

18 March

Many, many years ago today I was sad because Father died. But the sadness was very different then to the one I know now. I was young; I believed that there was joy on this earth. Today I know of no joy. The fear for that which I perceive as joy is too great. I know too much loss, too much self-deception. My children are definitely not happy, but I hope, so much, that they, the young, at least believe in the possibility of joy. The war goes on. The luck in the war is all on the other side.......will evil really triumph? Is it really the devil against God? There is much to think about. If there is a God, why shouldn't there be a devil? It all begins to frighten me. Don't both sides believe that God is on their side? Are they not all fighting for God and Country? Who admits to owing the devil allegiance? It appears that H and St and now also M are friends. Violence is what makes the difference. But violence like goodness and justice also comes from God. Henry – the dearest and best of all people is in love with a girl who apparently does not love him. So love also is not only to do with God but also with the devil. Senses, resistance and value are all dictated by love. Did the other woman love more and better than I? Why did she find joy with him when it would have meant so much more to me? The ways of God are unfathomable when they do not defeat the bad. And yet some people are at peace. I should like to walk in their shoes.

1 April

Bitter truth. Whatever fantasies I had 25 years ago about the future, no-one could have imagined this. One [Ada] detained against her will in the 'Diamond City' [Amsterdam], the other [Lisi] in Oxford, not freely but by a twist of fate. Neither can contact the other.

5 April

My first wedding anniversary. Fritz had things so much better than I all these years. Can one come back as someone else – I do not believe that. What I do understand, that I dare to say – I have hated. Perhaps it is sinful to say such things, but are all my sufferings in this life because of it? The general situation? Hitler and the others? Loneliness? My eyes? My nerves?

Myself? And yet it is spring in Oxford. Flowering shrubs and trees, flowers on the green grass, birdsong, gentle clear air.

4 May

I have had to endure many bad things. Illness – but it was because of the doctors – I have lost my belief in medicine. I can finally give up the hope that something can be done about my eyes. I am afraid of being alone, staying alone. I long for Mother, Emmy, and Max. All those I had but did not love enough. How much love would I give now, and how much would they take? Above all the fear of evil that seems to be more powerful than good. Poland, Finland and now Denmark – all in his hands. It does not look good in Norway. It all has nothing to do with right and justice, just the will of the more powerful. Lilli, were you right after all? Could you see further than me? Is hope worth anything? I still value it, but you didn't have any children. Ada and H.L.T. love each other. Can Ada love like I do? But if they cannot be together – it would be a good life for her. Vancouver, far away from the war, a home, her Thea, a loving son-in-law, a grandchild, friends, comfort, health. I am happy that such things still exist and that fate can change to good. But for me? I see nothing – but I shall wait.

5 May

One of the loveliest May days! Everything touched by mild gaiety. The air is balm. The majestic cedar tree outside my window dressed in green velvet and its tip touches the silver heavens. The chestnut tree reminds me of my childhood, of the tree in Angarten in the Neugasse in front of the window. Are its white candles lit? I long for home, Mother, love and childhood. I must not give voice to the pain that will destroy it all. Just to know once more what peace and happiness is before all the pictures pale into nothing forever.

7 May

There is no doubt, it all looks bad. Fighting in Norway, those who want to be neutral are turning away. Italy always aggressive. Ships being sunk. Never any news that is not depressing. My children, my beloved, splendid two….is it possible in this life that they should be thankless. How would I deserve that? Is it that each small sin, every mistake must be paid for? Never, never, never any reward!? But not all pay for their sins. That is the most awful; there is nothing left when belief has gone. Chaos, violence, pointlessness. Against this my children, honourable, clever, fair and industrious. He who really tries will be free. Is this still true?

15 May 1940

Norway has given up. The darkness closes in on us. Holland, Luxembourg, Belgium. Holland just capitulated … resistance was useless against the all-powerful evil. In Belgium they are still fighting. Is there still hope? This is what is going on all around me. And me? I do not want to know. Everyone is in danger. I cannot, will not think about it anymore. And that I am alone – is it my own fault? I will not think about it, I cannot. Lilli, Lilli, were you once again cleverer than me? – but you had no children. But you did believe in God – and still?

(The diary ends here.)

Translated by Antonia Brotchie

Appendix III: Flensburg Letter

From Henry Garton to his wife Jean,
written at 11 p.m. on 11 May 1945,
from somewhere in Northern Germany

I think I have passed the most eventful and interesting day, or two days, of my life and I could easily write a book about it, or still better a film, but I'll try to tell you just a little of what I have seen and done.

I left yesterday morning for Flensburg (a town quite near the Danish border) about 4 hours by car. Just another Captain (a radio technician) and myself, in order to take over the radio station there, which was still in German hands. Passed through Kiel, completely destroyed.

On the road we met ten thousand, if not a hundred thousand, German soldiers streaming south, home I suppose. Most of them completely exhausted, carrying or rather dragging along their belongings, practically in rags, some even without boots! Some pulling carts, some pushing wheelbarrows, some wounded, even on crutches. A few farm carts drawn by horses with women on them (in uniform, i.e. German A.T.S., or civilian). But many thousands of women marching along as well. On the roadside and in the fields crowds and crowds lying, completely exhausted. Among the marching even high officers, incl. naval and airforce, still trying to look smart, their chests covered with decorations. No picture of the retreat of Napoleon's 'Grande Armée' from Moscow could be worse. It was beyond description. Separated from them or sometimes even mixed with them marched freed 'slaveworkers', Russians, Poles etc and sometimes one hardly knew what was what. Apparently there was a lot of bloody fighting or rather killing going on, usually for the possession of a bike.

When we got near Flensburg the picture suddenly changed. We no longer saw any British troops or cars or

Military Police, but merely German sentries, fully armed and looking extremely 'business-like'. Crossings, bridges, etc were heavily guarded by German soldiers with steel helmets, automatic rifles, hand-grenades in their belts. When we got to the outskirts of Flensburg they even signalled us to stop, but we just drove past at top speed wondering whether we would hear shots fired at us.

We first drove to the transmitter outside the town, entered with drawn pistols in case of any funny business and informed the staff that we were taking over and that they had to stop broadcasting immediately. We then drove to the studio through a town packed with armed German troops and high-ranking officers, as smart as on a parade ground, heavily armed etc etc. We were more and more puzzled and did not feel too comfortable. We acted similarly at the studio and informed the two officers there, a Lieutenant and a Captain that at 3 pm (ie 15 minutes later) I would announce over the wireless that this was "Radio Flensburg, a station of the Allied Military Government". Just before 3 pm a Major appeared and told me he was sent by Gen. Kohlhauer, the *Reichsnachrichtenführer*, who would arrive in a few minutes to see me and asked me to postpone the announcement until then. I was getting more and more puzzled! Five minutes later a German General, accompanied by two other officers, full of red and gold trimmings, covered with decorations incl. the highest German order, the Pour le Mérit, around his neck, appeared, walked up to me, clicked his heels and saluted smartly!! I thought I was dreaming! He was trembling with nervousness and excitement (that humiliation must have been his darkest moment!) and explained that the German Government, ie Grand Admiral Dönitz had been given permission by Gen. Eisenhower to use this station only, for announcements by them in connection with the carrying out of the armistice terms.

To cut a long story short, I told him that I had to see that in writing, whereupon he said that if I followed him to the seat of the German Government he would ask Count Schwerin von

Krosigk, the new Foreign Secretary, to give me satisfaction! I began to be puzzled beyond description, until I found out that the present seat of the German Government was just outside Flensburg and that that General was a member of it and came from there. I also found out that Flensburg was only to be handed over next Sunday, that no allied troops would enter until then and that in the meantime the German troops remained armed. That explained everything, but we did not feel too happy by the thought that just we two had ventured ourselves among hundreds of thousands of armed German troops! Still, we went in the General's car to the Government buildings, a large building outside the town. Passed dozens of barriers guarded by German sentries pointing automatic rifles at us, but letting us pass and presenting arms when they recognised the Government sign in front and the General. It was all like Hollywood, sentries at the gates and doors, not even blinking with their eyelids, etc. We were led into the office of the Foreign Secretary (Schwerin von Krosigk) (there is still a Hitler picture on the wall) but both he and Dönitz were out. Anyhow we saw another Secretary of State and had a long conference, about which I will tell you another time. Then the General took us back to the radio station and after having censored the things he intended to broadcast, we departed.

That does not finish all the interesting experiences of the day. But the rest I can only tell you very briefly, I am too tired.

We wanted to spend the night in Denmark. That gave us a chance to see the German Army marching out of Denmark. We again saw tens of thousands, marching across the border in columns, partly still very smart, their rifles at the slope(!), partly somewhat less smart. Danish troops with machine guns pointed at them, keeping order and checking that they did not take with them things they shouldn't (all bikes were retained, thousands were stacked up!).

And then into Denmark, as far as Sonderborg, about 30 miles in. Thousands of flags, several in every window. People cheering us, many had not seen any Allied troops yet. When we stopped in the market place we were practically suffocated by the crowd. I had to give my autograph at least 100 times. Had a wonderful dinner, the best I had for 5 years, slept at a very nice hotel, walked through the town shaking hands left and right, being cheered etc. But still a lot of German troops there, saluting us terribly smartly!

Back today, further highly interesting sights at the frontier, in Flensburg, and on the way back. Was also on the last German aerodrome, saw hundreds of their planes still there, not yet taken over, and their staff there.

But I cannot write any more. Am falling asleep.

HKG

Appendix IV: Gerda

Gerda Lehman (née Königsgarten) was my father's first cousin who lived in Paris, whom I had met regularly in my childhood when she had visited my parents in London, and whom I knew my mother had continued to contact by phone for some years later. She was the only child of Ludwig, one of Ernst's elder brothers, who had taken over the family engineering business in Brno after Fritz had died. Gerda's mother had died when she was six. The engineering business was seized by the Nazis and 'aryanised' in 1940. In 1942 Ludwig had been deported to Theresienstadt and in 1943, after he had supervised the building of the railway line into the camp, he was transferred yet again, this time to Auschwitz where he met his end. Gerda, however, had moved to Paris and survived the war. This much I knew. At some stage she had obviously married a man by the name of Lehman, but who he was or what had become of him I never knew. He had never been mentioned, and whenever Gerda had visited us in London when we were children she had always come alone.

During the early years of my family research I had already made several attempts online to find the date of Gerda's death, and drawn a blank, and throughout the autumn of 2014, prior to finalising the text of my book, I made further attempts by contacting the Marie of the 16th arrondissement in Paris, but these too drew a blank. The reason, no doubt, was because although I had given a wide range of years for the search period, they were all prior to 2000, as I had never imagined she had lived to the ripe old age of 101. I had, not unreasonably, assumed that the reason my mother had lost contact with her many years ago was because she had died.

Nevertheless, the matter still plagued me, and in January 2016 I made yet another attempt by contacting the 'Service d'état civil de la Ville de Paris'. To my great surprise, and I do not know why, as I gave no more information than I had before, they came back with a copy of her death certificate showing she had only died in November 2013. This was of course a mixed blessing. On the one hand I was glad to have established when she had died, but I was mortified to have discovered that it was so recent and that I could therefore have easily visited her to discuss first-hand some of the places and events which I had written about in my book. Her input would have been invaluable. She might have been willing and able to have shed light on so much concerning our shared family's life in Brno, the family business, and even a first-hand description of my grandfather and great-grandfather. In all likelihood she had been born in the same house as my father and could have described it as it was in its heyday. The opportunity missed was galling and I felt shattered. Why had we lost touch with her? It was something I would probably never know.

The death certificate had given me the name of her late husband, but there were still many unknown facts which I might yet be able to get answers to: When did Gerda move to France and why? When did she marry Jacques Lehman and who was he? (The death certificate had produced his four Christian names, and from these he appeared to be French.) How had she met him and what became of him? Did he survive the war, and if not, how did Gerda manage to? How was her health in her final years? Did we lose touch with her because she had suffered from some kind of dementia? That seemed the most likely explanation, in which case I might have got no useful information from her even if we had met. Altogether, the situation was tantalising. But I resolved to get out of it what I could.

The first thing I did was to phone the office that had sent me the death certificate (part of the 16th Mairie), and when I asked about the two witnesses who were named in the certificate, the person I was speaking to knew one of them as someone who worked at the Hôpital Sainte-Périne. This was a tremendous lead. I googled it and discovered it was a hospital in the 16th arrondissement providing medical and geriatric care for the elderly, and it was only a few minutes away from Gerda's flat at 1, Square d'Urfé (an address I had always remembered as it was so unusual a name). I immediately telephoned them. They said they could not give me any information over the telephone, and they invited me to write to them. But that did not in fact get me any further. Despite repeated pressure from me, they claimed they could not give me any information without the authority of Gerda's 'proche' (her next of kin) and all they could do was forward a letter to her for her to reply to if she wished. They expressed sympathy for my position and said they would urge her to do so, inasmuch as they could.

    I waited for a reply, but to no avail - there came none. So I resolved to visit the Hôpital Sainte-Périne as soon as I could, and I determined to see what I could achieve with a bit of personal persuasion. I did not alert them I was coming as I did not want them to avoid meeting me, and in April I flew to Paris. I had decided to visit Gerda's old flat first before going on to the Hôpital Sainte-Périne afterwards, armed with all the information I could muster, including what I could discover from the present occupiers of her flat if I could meet them.

    A light drizzle was falling as I left the Metro station and I was horrified to realize that I had never visited her flat before, despite having lived in Paris for three months as a student in 1965. I do not know, to this day, why my parents had not insisted I visit her when I was there at that time. It is most odd. Perhaps however they did, and it was me who was not interested enough to do so. Again, I will never know. Still, I felt I was making up for it now, in some little way.

    I walked the hundred yards or so to her flat. I had checked it out several times on Google Streetview so it was almost as though I had been there before. It was one of several identical but grand blocks of flats looking over the Bois de Boulogne, and there was an array of bells on the door on which of course her name did not feature. But there was also a separate bell which I gathered from a passer-by was that of the concierge. I rang it several times and waited. Eventually, after about five minutes, the door opened and a woman appeared. She was clearly not the concierge, so I immediately engaged her before she had the opportunity to prevent me from entering, and asked her if she by any chance had known Gerda Lehman, who had been my father's first cousin. She replied straightaway that she had indeed known her, and known her quite well, and that furthermore she was about the only person in the building who had known her at all well, as she (Gerda) was a very difficult woman and had not endeared herself to others in the building! I gathered that her flat had not yet been re-let as there were still builders there renovating it, two years after her death.

By this stage I was inside the doorway, out of the rain, and had put my bag and my umbrella down, and I began to quiz this neighbour all I could. She explained that the concierge, who was Portuguese, was the only other person who had known Gerda well, but that she was on holiday for the week. She also said that I should not refer to her any more as a concierge – today they were called 'gardiennes', which was obviously considered less demeaning! But given my obvious age, she understood my mistake! I gathered that Gerda had moved to the Hôpital Sainte-Périne two or three times in the last years of her life as she had had several falls, but that she had remained fully compos mentis and in possession of all her faculties up until the time of her death. The neighbour, who was also Jewish, did not know how Jacques had died, nor how Gerda had avoided the round-ups during the war, but said that it was all a huge matter of luck as to whether one was caught or not. Gerda, like her, had obviously been lucky. The most useful fact I gathered was that Gerda had had a niece. As she had no siblings, this must have been a niece of Jacques, and perhaps she was the 'proche'.

I kept the neighbour talking as much as I could. She had an appointment to keep and so could not stand talking forever, so after a while I accompanied her to the Metro as we continued to talk, and there we parted. But she gave me the name of the gardienne and suggested I wrote to her to discover the name of the 'proche' who had taken care of Gerda's affairs. I could not believe my luck, that within minutes of arriving in Paris I had met a neighbour of Gerda's who had known her over many years, and I headed to the nearest bistro across the square where I enjoyed a wonderful soupe d'oignons and a cold beer and reflected on what I had discovered.

After lunch I went on to the Hôpital Sainte-Périne, a brief Metro stop away. There I visited the management office and explained my request, hoping that my presence would elicit more information than my earlier emails. But I was to be disappointed. They were adamant that they could give me no information at all, not even where Gerda was buried! When I enquired why, they said because I might be of a different faith and vandalise the grave! I told them I thought this was a bit ridiculous but they were adamant. But if you can't get information from the proper channels, there always remain the unofficial ones. I went back to the receptionist who operated the switchboard and said very plaintively that I was looking to find out where my great-aunt had been buried. She told me straight away that I could find out from the hospital morgue which was situated just next door! She also told me that the hospital records office could tell me what ward she had been in and the dates! The morgue had in fact just closed but it was anyway time for me to check into my Airbnb and I could come back in the morning.

The next day came and I was back at the morgue. The attendant didn't seem to be at all busy and did his best to dig out his old records but they didn't go back quite far enough, but he said he could make further enquiries and if I came back after lunch he would have the answer. So I headed off to the Mairie to see what they could tell me.

There again there was nothing more that I could ascertain about Gerda, so I went and had another onion soup, this time overlooking the Place de L'Etoile, and returned after that to the morgue. True to his word, the assistant had tracked down her burial place to Favières (Département 28). I was in business! I could think of no other reason for Gerda to be buried there other than that was where the niece lived. I had another lead to follow.

Before leaving the Hôpital, I visited the ward where Gerda had been when she died and tracked down the doctor who had been in charge, but not surprisingly she could not really remember Gerda after over two years, and anyway what could she have told me of her life or her family? But I felt that I had paid my last respects.

When I got back to my partner Bridget's holiday home in France, I contacted the Mairie in Favières and asked if they could let me know who had arranged the burial of Gerda Lehman in November 2013. By return of email, and without any hesitation, they told me it was a Muriel Le Barrois d'Orgeval and they gave me her address in Favières. When I subsequently phoned them to ask for her phone number, they said they did not have it, but that they had seen her only a few days before in the town and that she generally spent the summer there and the rest of the year in Paris. I was slowly making progress!

I tried to find a phone number for Muriel online, but without success. So I wrote a long and pleading letter to her, asking her to contact me. I also wrote to the gardienne of Gerda's old flat.

I felt I was rather more likely to hear from Muriel than the gardienne, but in fact it was a letter from the gardienne that arrived first. She told me that the only information she had from the notebook she kept was the telephone number of Gerda's niece, who was called Muriel (she did not know the surname), which was a Paris number, and a number for Gerda's sister-in-law, whose name she did not know. So now

I had it confirmed that Muriel was indeed the niece, and undoubtedly also the 'proche'.

Unfortunately the Paris number turned out to be a wrong number, but the sister-in-law's number was answered by a Caroline Dubruel who lived 18 kms south of Bordeaux. She was the niece of Gerda's sister-in-law (Jacques' sister Monique), who was now 95 and no longer of sound mind. Caroline had been living with her aunt for six years to look after her, but she was fascinated by my enquiry as she herself had been wanting to know more about Gerda, who had always remained a mystery as her aunt had always declined to answer any questions about her. There appeared to be some family rift or schism that made it impossible for her to obtain any information about either Gerda or Jacques. But there was a box of letters from Jacques in the house that she would be more than willing to share with me. Although she knew the name Muriel, as she remembers Muriel telephoning to inform her aunt of Gerda's death, she did not have any contact details for her, nor had she heard from her since. She told me that Gerda and Jacques had got married in Paris in about 1938 (she even had a photo of their wedding – as indeed I have), but that Jacques had become mildly schizophrenic thereafter. She believed that Jacques, who was ten years older than his sister – and therefore almost the same age as Gerda - , had died naturally in about the 1960s, and that Gerda had looked after him until his death. She had seen letters indicating that he had feared being identified as Jewish during the war, and had therefore obtained copies of his parents' and grandparents' baptism certificates (they had rejected their Jewish faith), in order to avoid being rounded up.

Caroline and her family had also always been puzzled as to what Gerda lived on, ie where her money had come from. They wondered if it had been some kind of reparations after the war (which I said I doubted), and there was some rumour that she had inherited some money from an uncle who was a writer. I said that that was also not possible, as far as I knew. But clearly the box of letters might answer a few questions and I arranged to call her again in a few days' time. Meanwhile I trawled the French online telephone directory again and decided to contact the few Le Barrois d'Orgevals that there were in Paris. I soon spoke to a Pierre Le Barrois d'Orgeval, who said he was the 'chef de famille' and knew all his relations, but that there was not a living Muriel among them! (His great-aunt however had been called Muriel, but she had died a few years ago.) He was as puzzled as I was about the Muriel in Favières!

Two days later I phoned the Mairie in Favières again to see if I could manage to get them by some ruse or other to find a phone number for her, and here I made my big break. They told me in fact that Muriel had now left Favières and, they presumed, returned to Paris. Although they also said they could not get her phone number, either there or in Paris, in the course of my conversation with them I established that Muriel was widowed, and I asked them if they knew the name of her late husband. With the help of someone who happened to be in the Mairie at that moment, they came back with the name Bruno. That turned out to be the key. Armed with that I searched the online telephone directory again to see if I could find Muriel's correct Paris number, and not only came up with the correct one for her Paris address (the gardienne had inverted two digits) but also a number for a house near Arcachon in the region of Bordeaux. I tried both numbers. The Paris one went to an answerphone, but the Arcachon one was answered by a boy's voice saying that Muriel was currently down at the beach but would be back later. I had tracked her down at last. But how would she respond when I called her back? I could not tell. Perhaps she would not even take the call.

The same boy's voice answered when I called back later that evening and I feared she would not come to the phone, but she did. When she asked me what I really wanted I referred to my various letters which I said I presumed she had received. She remained quiet, but did not deny it, and gradually while I continued talking she began to warm up. She told me she was not in fact a niece of Gerda's, but her god-daughter (it was sometimes easier to say she was her niece) – her mother and Gerda had been old friends. She thought Gerda and Jacques had met skiing in Austria before the war and they had married in Paris in 1939. Her father Ludwig had even come to the wedding, but he had not apparently been a very good father to her. She said he had rather neglected her and she had led a rather 'itinerant' life until she met Jacques, living in Germany and elsewhere.

Jacques' father Pierre was a 'négociant' in Bordeaux. The Lehman family apparently disapproved of Jacques' marriage to Gerda – they thought she was not smart enough for him, she had a foreign accent, she was over-dressed, coquettish, and wore too much make-up! Rather surprisingly they found her too provincial!

Jacques apparently developed his schizophrenia during the war and was in a home from the end of the war onwards. He died in the early 1960s.

As far as she knew Gerda and Jacques had spent the war years in Paris and seemed to do so without too much hardship. Gerda had said they 'went out often'. I asked what Gerda had lived on, and Muriel said she had had a pension from Jacques; but she was not wealthy and had not left anything substantial on her death. In fact, she said, her estate was negative. Nor did Gerda apparently have any photos or other memorabilia of her youth or her childhood in Brno. Muriel said she had cared for Gerda throughout the whole of her old age, and although she had heard of a cousin in London (my father or uncle) she had not known of my existence, and was surprised that I was suddenly taking so much interest when I had not done so during Gerda's lifetime. I tried to explain how this had come about, and I felt she began to understand, or at least gave the impression of doing so or she gave me the benefit of the doubt.

I thanked her profusely. It was a difficult conversation but I felt we ended on friendly terms and I felt I had gone just about as far as I could to fill my many unanswered questions. It is of course still a great regret that I had not tracked Gerda down before her death, the only person then still alive who had known the family house in Brno in its heyday.